Painting for Children

Painting for Children

A Collection of Paintings Done in the Classroom by Children from Five to Twelve

Lois Thomasson Horne

REINHOLD BOOK CORPORATION
A subsidiary of Chapman-Reinhold, Inc.
New York   Amsterdam   London

Mahalo nui loa
to The Kamehameha Schools,
to the children and teachers with whom I
have worked, and especially
to Bill and Anna

All photographs of children at
work by Luryier Diamond

33,343

Designed by Rosa Delia Vasquez
Printed by Halliday Lithograph Corporation
Color printed by Princeton Polychrome Press
Bound by William Marley Company
Published by Reinhold Book Corporation
430 Park Avenue, New York, N.Y. 10022

Contents

Credo   7

The Child and the Teacher   10

The Classroom:
Materials, Equipment, and Techniques   15

Motivation   23

Development   29

The Paintings   35
  Paintings by Five-year-olds   36
  Paintings by Six-year-olds   42
  Paintings by Seven-year-olds   56
  Paintings by Eight-year-olds   65
  Paintings by Nine-year-olds   77
  Paintings by Ten-year-olds   86
  Paintings by Eleven-year-olds   93
  Paintings by Twelve-year-olds   99

Index of Media   103

Index of Illustrations   104

Credo

Basically, the child looks out from the world of the self — the center of his private universe, *himself.* To the degree that he is sensitive to his surroundings and responds physically, emotionally, and intellectually, he enlarges his horizons in concentric circles of expanding consciousness. He sees, feels, thinks, and responds so that he is changed in some way. He becomes aware of who he is and where he is. He learns not only to fit into his environment but to simultaneously alter it to meet his particular needs.

A child needs to express himself and to communicate with others. He fulfills these needs most effectively in his own personal, creative statement or action. In this significant expression, tangible or intangible, overt or covert, a child is able to extend the self. The painting, poem, pot, sound, or action exists as a further dimension of the person who caused it to be. Its primary function is to state something that he needs to say; its primary importance is its meaning for him. But it has increased power and signif-

icance when it is shared with others and succeeds as communication.

Perhaps the most essential need of the human being is a feeling of self-worth. A positive reaction from others, recognition of his unique value, plus the achievement of communication reinforce the child's growing concept of himself. From the sense of accomplishment and self-realization through artistic expression comes a feeling of real satisfaction and joy. Experiences that result in articulation through art — through music, dance, drama, and all communicative and expressive thought — enrich and broaden the child's scope as an individual and as a member of society.

The child's creative statement is composed of both instinctive and acquired responses. On the one hand, his reaction to the environment is intuitive, unconsidered, and purely creative. He does things for reasons that he cannot explain, but that stem from an urge for expression which is part of his deepest self.

He identifies so completely with the animal, tree, or rock that he *is* animal, vegetable, or mineral. Thus he is the original artist in his direct, empathic, and natural oneness with the sense-stimulating elements of his surroundings.

On the other hand, the degree to which a child reacts is also conditioned by an accumulation of experience. His thought weaves constantly between the innate and the learned. It retains its identity while continually refocusing and changing: moving backward to memory and experience; forward to imagination, a world of possibilities and tangent ideas; inward to his subconscious faculties; and, finally, outward through some mode of expression — a word, song, dance, or painting.

The child's potentials for expression and communication through art should be continually nurtured and drawn out. Every child carries within him the basic capacity for art experience — his senses and intelligence. The definition of talent is often limited and circumscribing. It excludes or denies the fact that every child has something to say and can say it in a manner that makes it successful for him. The cultivation of awareness — an increased consciousness of everything that he sees, touches, hears, tastes, or smells — provides a springboard for perceptive response. A child who is allowed to exercise and develop his native capacities is receptive to a lifetime of real discoveries. He does not need to be stimulated by experiences that are arbitrarily and artificially structured by someone else. He finds for himself the patterns created in the sink by water and color, iri-

descent rainbows from drops of oil on wet streets, slithering raindrops on windshields and engine hoods — the infinite wonder of so-called ordinary things.

These responses are vitally important to the individual, both when he is alone with his emotions and thoughts and in his relationships with others. Sensitive responses equip him for enriched living, whether as active producer, user, or observer. In the final analysis, the latter two roles are not passive, but imply real involvement.

The impulse to explore, manipulate, and change media finds natural expression in painting. It can be developed, extended, and satisfied if opportunity and motivation are provided. The spectrum of painting includes enough possibilities for every child to find some method that will enable him to say what he has to say in his own way. In this book painting is presented in a broad sense and embraces the use of many kinds of color — wet and dry, thick and thin, transparent and opaque — applied by painting, printing, tooling, and texturing, on a wide range of surfaces — rough and smooth, absorbent and glazed, flat and raised.

The ultimate validity of a work of art, like that of an action or relationship, is in direct proportion to its meaningfulness for its creator and to the honesty of its conception and execution. It must be a true extension of its originator. A child brings his own private world into being through his art. The basic right of each individual to make his own statement, in his own terminology, must be understood and accepted as the premise for any creative relationship.

Painting experiences nourish a sensitive consciousness and sustain a natural dynamic growth. Painting can thus contribute to the development of every child, according to his potential, need, and interest. It can enable him to participate creatively in exploring and understanding the nature of art and equip him to enjoy the art of nature and the man-made world. Experiences in inventive use of all available materials enable him to express himself wherever he may be. Painting is a kind of visual Esperanto, providing a means for universal communication through symbol and image.

9

The Child and the Teacher

What happens to the child-artist during the process of his art experience — his flowering in what is basically a dialogue with himself — is also dependent on environment. The initial climate is determined by his parents, who influence his own ultimate evaluation of his efforts and achievements. Sympathetic and informed parents can either supply an invaluable supportive background for the child's art expression, or give him the feeling that his painting is of no value. Without being aware of it, parents may be bothered because the ideas expressed in the painting do not conform to their own. They should realize that the painting does not represent an actual thing at all, but rather the child's unique, subjective view of it. Through the realization that all paintings do not have to be comprehensible or pleasurable to him, the adult can come to an acceptance of the child's individuality and a recognition of his right of choice and interpretation.

The ideas and methods outlined in the following pages are based on the art program at The Kamehameha Schools in Honolulu, Hawaii, where the paintings in this book were done. At Kamehameha there are two other adults who are also deeply involved in the children's art experience: the classroom teacher and the specialized art teacher. Through cooperation and mutual support, we can help the child to achieve a more meaningful experience. The relationship is tremendously exciting and profitable for us as well.

Close contact is maintained between the two teachers and the students. At the end of each formal art period, tentative plans are projected for the additional time when the children will work with the classroom teacher before the next scheduled meeting. Projects may be continued or completed during this time, and any work started may be carried over into the following meeting with the art teacher. The two teachers work as a team and confer often. Immediately before each art class, the art teacher checks on the work in progress. When necessary, he can help

the classroom teacher to implement or plan additional classroom work involving art materials and techniques.

The classroom teacher is of vital importance — in many schools he must fill the role of art teacher as well. He is able to foster a continuing creative atmosphere by showing a lively interest in the child's ideas, generating excitement in planning and working, and expressing his appreciation and approval of the child's work; he effects the special blending of attitude and facilities that is conducive to freedom, exploration, and expression. Being present at the inception of many ideas and close to the sources of the child's interest, the classroom teacher must be alert to recognize and utilize the child's initial motivation. He knows the child intimately; he often understands and communicates with the child in a way that is impossible for an art teacher who comes in only at intervals.

The immeasurable value of the classroom teacher's interest, cooperation, and participation in the working situation does not depend as much upon his knowledge of art or his ability to teach it as upon his ability to generate vitality. He provides a continuing atmosphere of enthusiasm and concern. He is also an invaluable source of ideas, drawing upon the child's interests and the general curriculum in a way that the art teacher is unable to do. At the same time, the classroom teacher who works with the specialist has the opportunity to learn techniques he can use when the specialist is not available, as well as to observe and work with the child in a new context.

The art teacher contributes a more comprehensive background in art. He provides a continuous in-service training that keeps the classroom teacher aware of trends and new ideas in art. He acts as a reservoir of resources and technical knowledge, and can offer a wide range of suggestions about the overall goals desired for and by the child. In addition, the art teacher introduces a new viewpoint, and may see aspects of the child's work that are not evident to the classroom teacher. Two heads, two hearts, two approaches, and two sets of eyes, ears, and hands implement the goals set by each and by both.

The art teacher must possess a rich background of knowledge and experience supported by an understanding of children and their development. He must be imaginative, flexible, and empathic in order to awaken the child to his own potential and help him explore and expand it. He must preserve the purity of the child's intuitive response while allying it with intellectual refinement and technical knowledge. Setting the stage, fostering heightened awareness and response, challenging thought, and implementing individual expression are the art teacher's function. His role is never the same for any two students or occasions, and thus he is continuously involved in an innovative, creative activity himself. This is what makes teaching art so fascinating, demanding, and rewarding.

Not all working classroom situations are the same, of course. They would be static and boring to all the participants if they were. Taking into account the multiple factors involved in the learning-teaching situation, the inspired teacher examines, evaluates, and constantly revises his approach to art instruction. Ideally, the basic philosophy and teaching procedure of the art teacher are so intermeshed that neither can be stated or put into effect without the other. There are, however, instances in most teaching situations when it is necessary to adjust to limitations of time, space, facilities, objectives, and so on. But if it is not always possible for the teacher to practice what he preaches, he should know why he cannot, and should objectively examine himself and the situation to see what changes can and must be made.

The teacher should be in command without over-directing or overanticipating the results. He may suggest, but the child should be free to accept or reject. The teacher is the director, but at the same time he is an assistant and one of a working group. He must sense when the child needs the contact and interchange that will widen his horizons and quicken his imagination, and he must know when to supply the impetus a child needs to move ahead. Through their dialogue, the teacher can help the child focus his attention, articulate his questions, and find answers.

The teacher must also be able to help the child understand and accept temporary disappointments. It is an accomplishment for both teacher and child when a rather awkward, blustery eight-year-old can shrug his shoulders philosophically as the two attack the job of cleaning up a painting that is partially flooded by a lake of tempera islanded with broken glass. Such an achievement is underscored when that child says, with a communicative grin, "Well, I guess

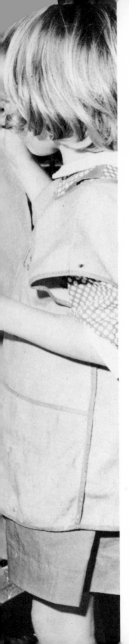

it's just not my day," or, "That looks like an octopus; I can make it into a deep-sea picture."

The child should be a "sender" and not merely a passive receiver, a trained performer. There can and must be a vital communion between the art teacher and his student — an elusive sense of understanding and empathy that may or may not be expressed in words. The relationship is real and personal. Its existence cannot be taken for granted, because it comes into being during the process of communication. Its most important feature is that it is subject to change, and the steps taken in this voyage together are determined during the actual process.

A child often asks questions to establish contact with the teacher. He will ask where to put his painting, where to find the sponges, or other questions to which he knows the answers. This is a device to attract attention, but it often expresses the child's need for his presence to be acknowledged. "Here I am," he is saying. "Pay attention to me, love me." A question such as "What color shall I make the tree?" should be referred back to him; for instance, the teacher might ask, "What color do you think would go well with the colors you have already used?" It is important to establish a warm (but sensible) rapport so that when the student has a problem, he will be relaxed and confident about asking for help. The tone of the classroom should be happy and comfortable but also serious regarding the value of what is being done. An essential element in the teacher-child relationship — its "sunlight" — is genuine but discriminating mutual appreciation: genuine because the child can sense any false note, and discriminating because the objective of child and teacher is growth.

The child must know that his work gives pleasure: the teacher must be genuinely excited about what he does. Lack of understanding or appreciation generates a negative and restraining atmosphere. The teacher supports the child and helps him to realize and value his individual style of expression by believing in his latent potential. This is expressed by a sincere, positive attitude toward what the child has to offer at each stage of development. The teacher who truly responds to originality automatically provides a wholesome climate. He not only supplies the child with the materials, equipment, and techniques needed, but also gives him the fullest opportunities to use them.

Whenever possible, the teacher should take the time to really see and enjoy with the child the successive stages of a painting, and he should show further recognition by posting paintings. Some students also find it helpful to have a place where they can post work in progress: this offers a continuing opportunity for eye and mind to explore possibilities for further development. Such work may be temporarily taped to the chalk rail, on a door, etc. In order for the child to feel successful in expressing himself in his own way and, in time, to be able to evaluate his work in terms of his own potential, he may be introduced to the work of other artists — for instance, those with whom he has something in common or whose style is recognized because it is particularly individual.

With such help, the child can learn to use and en-

joy his sensitivity, increase his ability to respond, quicken his visual perception, and come, gradually, to see the elements and principles of art in his environment, his work, and the work of others.

Instructors who are fortunate enough to work with the same child for a long time can arrive at a comfortable, satisfying, and productive working relationship. At Kamehameha the art teacher works with the same children for three to six years. Consequently, their rapport is progressively increased and strengthened, giving the teacher a tremendous advantage in knowing how to meet the demands, encourage the explorations, and challenge the inventiveness of each individual. This approach takes time, but it is stimulating and exciting, and it is vitally important because it brings about a direct and deep involvement on both sides of the relationship.

The Classroom:
Materials, Equipment, and Techniques

Physically, the only requirements for painting are receptive surfaces, media, and tools or equipment for application. In the classrooms at Kamehameha these basic facilities are maintained primarily by the classroom teacher and the students. They provide mainly for drawing and painting with various media and making simple constructions with paper and wood.

As is commonly evidenced on sidewalks, walls, memo pads, beaches, and all inviting and convenient surfaces, drawing is a basic, necessary, and fruitful activity. It develops the individual art vocabulary and whets the child's ability to see. It increases his consciousness of what is around him and helps him to utilize aspects of the environment for his personal expression.

Recognizing this need and urge to draw, we give the children the chance to scribble, doodle, and record their ideas at all times. A variety of drawing tools — pencils, crayons, india ink, small brushes, and sticks are always available in the classroom or on the "art cart." As in painting, the children are not actually taught to draw but are provided with continuing opportunities and incentives for drawing. It is understood implicitly that one person's sketch does not have to comply with anyone else's idea of drawing. Extended experiences in drawing help to establish and clarify the direction or content of immediate work, and many children choose to make small sketches or notations as preliminaries to painting. A collection of the student's sketches and drawings often serves him as a resource portfolio of ideas.

Tempera paint, wax, oil, and watercolor crayons, paste, three kinds of painting paper, newsprint, and colored papers also are always available; in addition, each classroom is provided with chipboard work boards, water containers (often shallow cans), small cut sponges, and three to four dozen widely varied sizes of short-handled bristle brushes. (All brush handles are sawed down to eight- or nine-inch lengths to make them easier to manipulate and prevent tilting over of paint containers.) These supplies are restocked from a common, open-stock storeroom. This center also contains a variety of paper in sheets and rolls, colored construction and chart paper, tissue paper, waxed paper, etc., and it offers findings such as tin cans, aluminum-foil plates, sand, sawdust, shells, seeds, boxes, and scraps of cloth.

Items needed for special work and not provided in the open storeroom can be obtained by request or are brought in by the art teacher. These include watercolor sets, opaque-color palettes, felt-tip markers, dyes, polymer or latex paints, and equipment for sewing, clay work, printing, weaving, metal work, and mosaic. It is not always possible, of course, to provide and use a scope as wide as we would like, but we offer as many choices as possible at each level for use within the art program as well as in leisure time.

Each classroom has some storage space in the sink area for brushes, sponges, and paints and several shallow drawers for paper and paintings. Finished and unfinished work is stored separately so that work in progress can be located easily. Although there may be variations from room to room, each has a counter, a small table, a set of trays, or a cart where twenty-five to thirty-five containers of paint are kept at hand. These paint jars (baby-food jars, plastic containers, etc.) are all the same size so that they can all be covered with a piece of cardboard. They contain small amounts of paint so there is less to clean up if one is turned over or dropped, and to keep the colors fresh and clear.

Many types, shapes, and sizes of paper and other surfaces are available to work on: zest is added through tactile and visual stimulation. The rough finish of natural screen milling paper is inviting for chalk work, wet or dry, and it actually works to "sand" the chalk from the stick. Smooth, glazed finger-painting paper makes a perfect gliding surface for felt markers and sticks or cotton swabs dipped in ink. Because it reflects light, white drawing paper enhances the brilliance of transparent watercolor. Such surfaces as pages from newspapers and glossy magazines, corrugated paper, and waxed paper all have qualities that appeal to touch as well as sight (they even sound different). Pencils, pens, sticks, and other implements are used for small work surfaces, and brushes of all sizes, brayers, sponges, sprayers, fingers, and hands for larger areas.

The students work with all the materials and equipment available, as well as anything they can invent. Tempera, watercolor, chalk, finger paint, latex paint, dye, pencil, marker, ink, charcoal, and many kinds of crayon (wax, oil, watercolor) are used at all levels. The older children also use melted crayon, oil paint, polymer, and enamel. Since the overall quantity of paint remains the same no matter what colors are used, the basic color range is supplemented by dark shades of blue, red, and green, as well as by a wide variety of unusual colors, including ochre, gray, lavender, maroon, yellow-orange, magenta, burnt sienna, and turquoise. There is a marked contrast between the students' reactions to painting with a limited range of dull colors and their responses to a wide, more provocative palette.

A constant alertness to sources of free materials — "findings" and "throw-aways" — allied with the inventive use of all kinds of stuff make it possible to allot more of the art budget to materials of the best quality that is possible and practical. Flyers sent to parents bring in a constant stream of all kinds of interesting things to vary the painting experience: small paper cuttings from print shops, cloth scraps, foil, lace, wood scraps, paper doilies, colored earth, beach sand, chopsticks, toothpicks, yarn, corks, bottle caps, glitter, buttons.

The techniques used for application of the media are varied: they include painting with many sizes and types of brushes, several printing processes, tooling or scratching painted areas, and cutting and pasting to build up surfaces with cloth, yarn, paper, etc. If limitations of facilities and space make it impractical to use several painting media simultaneously, the possibilities of one medium may be extended. For example, tools such as sticks, yarn, printing objects, or fingers might be tried, and excursions in blotting, dripping, and blowing offer different approaches to painting with tempera. The children are encouraged to find many ways of applying the media to the surface. The method is determined by the student (unless it is deliberately destructive). He might, for instance, be shown that certain uses of a brush are less wearing than others, but if he needs to pounce the brush, he *needs* just that. He may be provided with special brushes for the purpose, or left alone.

Preliminary pencil drawing on the painting surface itself is not encouraged: the lack of compatibility between the size and character of a pencil and a brush often results in the loss of the quality of the pencil and a limitation of the potentialities of the brush.

At appropriate times, materials and techniques are described so that the students understand their character. If it is necessary to give demonstrations, they are technical illustrations of the properties and potentials of the material or technique. Any design resulting from a teacher or student demonstration is always signed to make it clear that repetition of it is copying.

A discussion based on questions such as the following might precede the use of a medium or follow a child's discovery of a possible use for it: What is this (a crayon)? What is it made of? How was it made? Have you used it before? How have you used it? Can you think of other uses? What would happen if it were heated? cooled? mixed with water? How do you think it could be melted or dissolved? What happens when it is applied lightly? heavily? to a rough surface? to a smooth surface? to a porous surface? when it is covered with watercolor? with another crayon? Why does it react the way it does in each case?

Whenever possible, the student learns about media by using them himself. He learns by actually painting and making his own discoveries, not by watching someone else. On-the-spot identification and analysis of technical problems result in a per-

sonal knowledge of what works and what is apt not to work.

The potentialities of media can be discovered through deliberate investigation and experimentation, but accidental happenings often provide information and present provocative possibilities. The "accident" may be intentional, as when a student is deliberately exploring, or it can "just happen." If the child is alert to the unexpected, he can use it immediately or file it away as technical knowledge for later work.

The experiments that don't work can serve as useful negative knowledge, and seemingly unfortunate accidents can have positive results. An otherwise discouraging picture on which paint has been spilled might be turned into a new treatment of the original idea or a totally new idea. A problem-solving approach, such as a game of association or identification, can result in the use of an unintended effect as the point of departure in a new direction. Experimental excursions into the use of paint, such as dripping, blotting, blowing, scratching, and smearing, are often triggered by accidents.

New work problems are related to positive and negative knowledge gained in previous experiences. The opportunity to use a new medium or technique is challenging and stimulates ideas. New processes are gradually added to the child's repertory, and opportunities for exploration and variation are provided whenever feasible, to maintain the dynamic tension of excitement and discovery. For instance, children who have done a lot of tempera painting will probably welcome a change of pace and respond with enthusiasm to the novelty of using mixed media, making tissue-paper laminations, or combining paint and collage.

When the interest is sustained, an activity may be pursued in depth. For example, a ten-year-old who shows a strong interest in printing is encouraged to explore every possible method of printing. He will have done prints with sticks, found objects, string, glue designs, and simple collages, and he is ready to learn other techniques, such as block printing with linoleum or wood, including multicolor overprinting done by cutting away the block progressively or building up a design with several blocks, simple intaglio, screen printing, extensions in brayer printing, or combinations of these techniques. He can use any of the printing processes on prepared surfaces such as collages or on partially painted papers.

Work areas may be desk or table tops, but many children prefer to work on the floor. Several desks or tables are sometimes pushed together to provide a large work surface or arranged in clusters for group work. Often all the furniture is pushed aside to create open floor space. In good weather, additional space is provided by an adjoining hallway or open *lanai* (porch).

This irregular "moving day" method lends an element of novelty to the daily routine. Although the scene may seem to an observer to lack organization, the procedure results in a happily relaxed working atmosphere. It provides for exchange and social intercourse between large or small groups, as well as privacy for those who desire or need it. Privacy does not require a private carrel or enclosure providing complete physical isolation, but may be achieved by the simple expedient of using a corner nook, making a pocket in which to "disappear" behind a desk, locating a work area out of the traffic pattern, or simply turning one's back on the movement and action of this busy microcosm.

Social adjustment is necessary in a working situation where there are twenty-five or more children and one or two instructors bounded by the spatial limitations of a regular classroom equipped with one sink. To provide a general overall procedure, and reduce the amount of orientation necessary, organization of materials and equipment and the rules for preparation, use, and clean-up are basically the same in all the classrooms.

Children can understand that some guidelines are desirable not only as a communal convenience but from a personal standpoint, and they can accept the necessary limitations. It is easy for them to develop basic work habits because they can see that it is both logical, practical, and in the end more pleasurable to have equipment and tools in good order and supplies readily available. They soon learn that it is distracting to interrupt an interesting activity to locate some item which is not in its assigned place; they then understand why the paints and brushes are in a specific place in the classroom. They recognize that in a group situation there can be more freedom of action within a general, democratic framework than with no regulations. It is logical for procedure to be determined by those involved, according to surroundings, equipment, and activity. When the students as a group exercise maximum control over the working situation, it helps to develop their sense of responsibility without taking away their freedom to function autonomously.

For example, a classroom experience with badly treated work boards showed that it was not very enjoyable to have to work on bumpy, crooked surfaces. This was a problem the children could solve: they determined how the boards got that way and where and how they could be stored to prevent further warping. Once this was established, everyone could find a work board when he needed it, and put it away when he finished working.

When several brushes were left bristle down in a container over the weekend, the bristles were set permanently out of shape. The children realized that it was necessary to choose between using unsatisfactory brushes and learning to store them so that the bristles remained straight. Another class had to decide, as a group, whether it was preferable to wash sponges as they needed them during a work period or to keep sponges clean by washing them after each use.

The object is to achieve a judicious balance between freedom and discipline. For example, one of the general rules is that a child may put his work board on the floor anywhere in the room except immediately in front of the sink. If he works there anyway, he cannot legitimately complain if he or his work gets spattered with paint or water. Every child knows that he may cooperate with another child to produce a painting or perhaps help a classmate paint part of

his painting (usually a background area and not a part of the *idea*), but he must *never* work on another child's painting without an invitation.

During the initial planning period for an activity or with the introduction of new materials or techniques, work procedures, lists, references, vocabulary, and other details are sometimes written on the blackboard, where they may be referred to as needed. This information may also be put on film to be used on the overhead projector, and it can be kept as long as the work is in progress. This makes it easy for class or individuals to review. Work periods are generally prefaced by a quick résumé of previously planned procedure so that everyone knows what to do. Thus, once work begins, the mechanics create as little diversion as possible.

In order to avoid congestion in the sink area at the end of the work period, children are encouraged to keep their work areas and equipment clean as they work. If a child finishes his painting and has a short interval of time, he can make a sketch for a new painting, help another child, do general clean-up, read, or pursue other interests.

Generally it is a good idea not to have too many children involved at one time in the general clean-up. Many class groups have found it very effective for individual students to take turns in assuming responsibility for overseeing the general work habits and maintenance of supplies for a given period. Other students who assume special jobs, such as washing brushes, filing paintings, and mopping the floor, check with this student. Since they all take charge in turn, the authority of the student in charge is usually respected.

When there is only one sink (or in instances when buckets of water are used), it is more practical, at the end of the painting session, to put all the soiled brushes bristle down in a container, such as a gallon-sized plastic bleach bottle with the top cut off, and let one or two children wash all the brushes at one time. Brush-washing can also be done quietly at some time later during the school day. Cleaning up is sometimes made into a game by counting the number of paint spots that each member of a small group can scrub up or by winding up the tag ends of a cleaning period with a count down.

One note about classroom procedure may be added here. Accidents are a part of many creative activities. The simple, basic rule that applies to other accidents is equally valid for the classroom: If you aren't involved and can't lend constructive assistance, keep out of the way!

Motivation

Painting, like all art, has its roots in experience and imagination, and is prompted by the stimulation and interaction of all the faculties of the artist. The child's experiences should not be compartmentalized, but synthesized. Rich new tones and shades of meaning are patterned by interweaving all the experiences that make up the total child. At Kamehameha art is related to language, social studies, science, mathematics, and every field in which the students are involved. We strive to help them to see that there is a relationship between art and science or art and music and to perceive basic underlying principles common to all three.

Each child's statement is, however, made within the boundaries of his psychological environment. He is stimulated to creative thought and action through experiences that further his awareness, through inquiry, exploration, and observation. The inspiration — the first step in the realization of a painting — may originate from one source or a combination of sources: the child himself, his participation in a group activity, or mental or physical stimulation that are the result of a scene or situation designed for pupil interaction.

Some children come to their first painting period with definite ideas about what they wish to paint; others bring in souvenirs from summer activities or are interested in a beehive or ant colony from the science center, or know we need place mats for the lunch tables. We can take off from or zero in on any idea that catches the imagination. For instance, the word *summer* could bring to mind other images such as picnicking, swimming, hiking, fishing, flying, boating, visiting friends, or other exciting experiences that can act as stimuli for painting; the word *ocean* might serve as motivation for a mural about things that live and grow in the sea, and so on. A word, gesture, or sound can act as a point of departure for a series of impressions and relationships. The original concept may be expressed in the final statement,

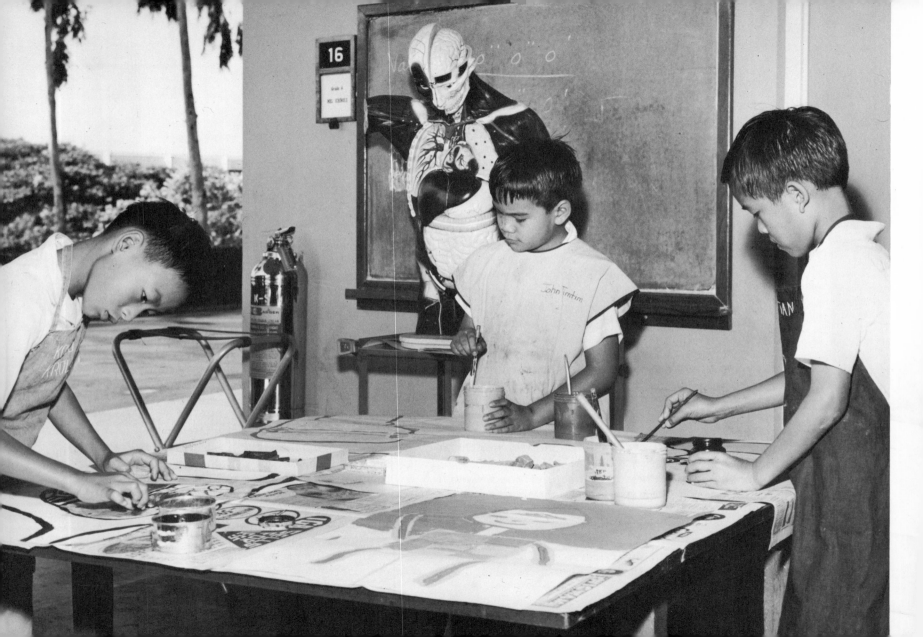

or it may evolve into something quite different through a chain reaction of associations and mutations.

In all art work, including projects connected with a specific area of study, desire for involvement and discovery are of first importance. The project itself acts as a catalyst for the interpretation of facts or expression of feeling. Thus, a painting stemming from a science unit is art inspired by scientific knowledge and not a detailed, factual rendering. It is the child's own translation of the subject matter, expressed in his own terminology.

The students blow bubbles or create rainbows with a prism and open up a new vista for inquiries about color and light that can be answered through painting. Projecting colored light on a painting or looking at it through a sheet of colored film, they achieve a monochromatic effect and observe how colors are changed by light. Working in a blacked-out room, in one of our explorations of color and light, the children discover that some contrast of light and dark is necessary for them to see form. Following this observation by painting in semidarkness, they find that their ability to see their work is determined by the contrast of values in the paintings and the amount of light in the room.

Provocative questions can prompt children to stretch their imagination or stimulate them to see things from a new physical perspective. What do you think is in this sealed box? What would you put in the box? If you could fly, what would our campus look like? What would you see in a cross section of a passenger plane, hotel, submarine, pineapple, car motor?

In a vicarious experience such as the study of the Stone Age, the child's natural urge to dramatize can be brought into play. Let him imagine himself in a situation where his very existence depends wholly upon his ability to hunt. When he is aware that he would have to be able to kill the beasts which provide his main source of food and clothing with his bare hands and the rude weapons he has made, he has a graphic picture of how, through actual physical contact, he would know the qualities of the animal — the vicious jaw, piercing tusks, sharp hooves, and the powerful shoulders and back. With this empathic knowledge, the child is able to really appreciate cave painting. He can then, in his role of primitive man, make his own painting using charcoal and soot which he has made, earth which he has gathered, and selected colors of chalk.

The approach of make-believe is effective with all age levels. The teacher can help the children to imagine what it was like to sail with Columbus, to live in ancient Greece, or to be an Australian Aborigine. By pretending to be a dinosaur, a worm, a space man, a streak of lightning, the child is able to express graphically his feeling about these things.

The teacher must not only be alert to motivational possibilities as they occur, but must also be able to design environments that prompt the child to respond. For example, the child might get an idea for another painting from the feathery, branching effect he discovers when one color he is using bleeds into an adjacent color. On the other hand, the response might stem from a similar but planned experience in observing the effects made by dropping concentrated inks or dyes into a shallow container of water or onto a wet paper surface. Either of these experiences in perception and sensory awareness could extend to further observations (made by the student on his own or prompted by the teacher), such as seeing similar designs in bare trees, leaf skeletons, river systems on maps, or the lines in the palm of the hand.

The art program can gather momentum if groundwork has already been prepared in the classroom by the teacher and his students through study, discussion, reports, movies, excursions, and other activities that *demand* translation into the child's own terms. When the art teacher enters the scene, there will usually be a lively brainstorming session. Individual or group art work can be motivated by recalling or anticipating experiences, by expressing immediate reactions to a current stimulus, and by using the imagination.

An experience is most effectively expressed at the peak of the impetus, when the wave of enthusiasm carries it to the most pertinent conclusion, but interest in a special subject, such as horses, hot rods, or ships, may be pursued over a prolonged period. Group plans may originate with any of the individuals involved: the participants move into and away from the center of attention. Suggestions offered by teacher or student are like seeds, which are sown with the tacit understanding that they can be considered, used, or discarded.

Working within a particular frame of reference can, at times, be the most desirable as well as the most feasible method of motivation. For instance, during orientation at the beginning of the year or when the class is large, it can be as effective as it is expedient to work with a limited range of media — one color of ink or tempera might be offered, with a choice of tools including pens, brushes, sticks, Q-tips, and straws. A change of pace in painting can result from working with one medium on different shapes and sizes of paper — long strips, circles, triangles, free forms, and shapes with holes in them. If the painting area is not ready or the art period is too short to use wet media, provocative materials such as newspaper, sandpaper, onionskin, paper towels, cloth scraps, and carbon paper can make work with crayons exciting.

Our goal is to take the child as far as he can go with interest and understanding. We want him to find out things for himself as much as possible, so we don't tell him too much, but try to provoke his curiosity. Whenever possible, he is guided to see relationships or contrasts: he is urged, for example, to compare the art of primitive peoples he studies — American Indians, ancient Hawaiians, cavemen, Australian Aborigines, etc.

Although it may be more desirable to follow motivation and planning with a long painting period, short class periods or tight schedules can make this impossible, and therefore the activity must be conceived so that it can be done in stages. Discussion, research, sketching, preparation, and setting up of

work might be done in one or two beginning phases, and subsequent periods of individual or group work be allowed for the execution of the project itself.

Teacher and children can quickly and easily establish the work procedures necessary for one activity; new procedures and explanations concerning the preparation, use, and care of materials are introduced as necessary. Gradually, individual students and small groups can move from one activity to any other for which materials and facilities are available. If the ideas for possible activities are listed and winnowed down to a feasible number, the children — individually, in committees, or in groups — can make their choices and voluntarily assume responsibility for the projects they undertake.

Work usually continues as planned, but at times a special event will bring about a change of direction or cause work in progress to be temporarily shelved. This sidetracking is done with the understanding that the work that is in abeyance will be completed later. There is a happy and necessary flexibility in this rule.

Sometimes it would be useless and frustrating for a child to have to continue work on a painting. Basically, however, it is demoralizing not to carry problems through to satisfying solutions. When a teacher knows his students well, he is able to sense whether a child should continue his work, have a short rest from it, or make a complete break.

It often happens that a painting cannot be completed and must be continued at another time. This is usually not desirable, but the interval, which might be thought of as a dormant period, can actually be a time of maturation and unconscious growth. The child returns to his unfinished work with fresh energy and "new eyes." The areas he has painted are dry and ready for overpainting, patterning, elaboration, or other changes. He may wish to continue in the original direction, or the interim may have provided him with new ideas. The extension of the work time, and, consequently, of the child's attention span, can bring out a capability he did not realize he possessed.

Development

The art program at Kamehameha is prefaced by a statement of our philosophy and our objectives and planned around a flexible framework of experiences and processes. This guide, constantly being examined in the light of new knowledge about the learning process and human behavior, lists the experiences and objectives that we feel should be continuous at all levels of development and those that are designated for specific levels. Mural painting, for example, is listed at all age levels, with some indication of the types most suitable for different levels. Thus, making a composite mural by joining individually painted parts, the simplest method, is as valid for the twelve-year level as for the five-year-old, although the older child can use more sophisticated techniques and arrangements. On the other hand, work with oil or polymer paint is usually done only by the older children.

We keep in mind an overall view of all the experiences that we want to introduce and offer them when-ever they coincide with the individual motivation of the children or classroom interests, or seem especially meaningful. Any medium or technique is good whenever it is keyed to the needs of the child. What the experience means for him is more important than whether he has it in September or May.

At the beginning of the school year, the teacher's procedure in motivating a six-year-old may be different from that used with a ten-year-old due to the nature of each child's background experience, interests, and vocabulary, but interpretation of idea and use of materials by each child depends upon his stage of development rather than how old he is. Later in the year, the teacher will adjust the stimuli to the changes in each child as he increases his fluency of ideas and extends his experience in working with media, but the response of each to motivation will continue to be geared to his individual level of development.

First experiences with media are exploratory and

manipulative. This approach is natural, and it is desirable at all levels. By seeing, touching, and, on occasion, smelling, tasting, and hearing, the child becomes acquainted with materials and equipment. As soon as he is ready, their use is expanded and developed in consecutive experiences and techniques.

The paintings of the five-year-old are done primarily with tempera thick enough to be easy to control. As he becomes more competent in the use of the brush, the applications of the paint become progressively varied. The child learns to paint with a variety of types and sizes of brushes and with other tools, including sponges, sticks, and printing equipment such as brayers, corks, and spools. He learns gradually to use washes and thin solutions, to spatter, drip, and trail the medium, to control overpainting on both wet and dry surfaces, and to use drybrush techniques.

A child who is trying oil paint for the first time will want and need to thoroughly investigate the medium. He may feel the consistency of the color by squeezing it from the tube and rubbing or smearing it with his fingers, and he may smell the oil of the pigment base and the turpentine thinner. He should have the opportunity to try the medium on various types of paper, cloth, wood, and other surfaces. Through these experiences he will learn about the body of the paint, its viscosity and plasticity, and some of its blended or surface effects.

Children often repeat these investigations at the beginning of a work period, especially when a medium is used at intervals. In finger painting, a highly tactile experience, there is nearly always a reaction to the texture (consistency) and temperature of the mixture, an enjoyment of the feel of it on the fingers and the sensation of the hand gliding on the slippery surface.

During the scribbling, exploratory stage, the child is less apt to see the potentials of what he does. Since his involvement is primarily kinetic, he may continue painting until he has a scramble of mud-colored pigment, and he may be quite satisfied with this. Later, when he has begun to organize his color-shapes in space, he may not be content to leave this dull mass, but will go on, using it as a background for contrasting colors, scratching it to create texture, or overpainting it when it has dried. A young child may unconsciously select colors and shapes that produce mood or express feeling. An older child will consciously and deliberately use his colors and shapes to translate his idea into form and content; he can produce a predetermined effect.

The children learn by working with media and techniques. For example, we offer them a wide range of colors. When a student wants a specific shade or an unusual color, he mixes it. As he uses the paint, he learns to decide what color he needs: he considers what he has already used, reviews the possibilities, and determines whether it is preferable to repeat or select another for contrast. By the time the children are twelve, they have done a great deal of painting and become fairly proficient in the use of tempera and other media. They have learned to mix

31

the colors they need. They know something about using contrasting colors and values and have some idea of the relationship of color and mood.

This fact-finding or discovery approach is significant and rewarding. The knowledge gained serves as a basis for a repertory to be used in subsequent work, and it results in extended awareness and individual aesthetic sensibility. In addition, during the search for relevant information and through experiential learning, the child builds up a supportive vocabulary. For example, a five-year-old finds that when a thin solution of tempera or finger paint is put over a partially crayoned surface, the liquid does not stick to the crayoned areas. This technique, which our younger students prefer to label *magic painting,* is the first of a series of experiences with resist. The child later learns that the process can be varied by adding more crayon to parts of his painting, by overpainting with ink, felt-tipped markers, or additional paint, and that resist painting can be done with dye on cloth. During these sequential experiences, he learns to properly describe them as *resist* techniques. He has also been exposed from the beginning to pertinent words such as *absorbent, overpaint, background, contrast, wash,* etc., and gradually these become a part of his art vocabulary.

Initial play accomplishes little unless it is soon paralleled by an alertness to discoveries, both intentional and accidental. These discoveries, consciously used or rejected, form a personal working vocabulary and serve as the nucleus for the development of individual style. The child moves toward an expression of order that is meaningful to him (though not necessarily to others). Continued involvement results in the invention of personal symbols and images for concepts and experiences; these may be abstract or schematic rather than visually factual. The child should be encouraged to find and use his own visual terminology. He should be assured that he is the "boss" of his painting and that he can use any color he likes, because it is a *painting* of a thing, not the real thing. With growth, he can develop clearly structured forms that show his increased awareness of the character of his subject matter or the nature of his experience.

When a child begins to paint, his precise idea or intention may not be clearly defined, and the statement he makes may not necessarily have a definite meaning for him. Whatever degree of visual realization takes place, however — whether the painting succeeds in expressing an idea or not — is not of essential importance. The painting *is* — it exists as an extension of the child, and its value is based not so much on what it is but on what has happened to him: whether he has widened his visual perception, gained new knowledge, increased his ability to work independently and confidently, grown in social responsibility.

Each child has his own personal vision and rate of development. For instance, although he may show consistent use of schematic forms in painting, when he finger-paints he may be satisfied to manipulate the medium without achieving any clear design. Whatever a child's level of performance, it is personal and usually right for him, and it should not be related to his chronological age except as a matter of observation. He must at all times be assured that he is accepted and valued *as he is,* and allowed to work at his own level.

If a child is unhappy with what he is doing, he may need technical help in selecting projects that satisfy him, or guidance toward an appreciation of the value and artistic quality of his work. (If a child is emotionally or physically upset, his painting is often affected noticeably: he is not as imaginative, nor does he succeed in expressing his ideas as effectively as usual.) When a child asks for specific help or the teacher senses that it is needed, he should be given an opportunity to see, touch, act out, or perhaps just talk about the things he is trying to depict. This will help him sharpen his perception and bring his idea into focus. If he wishes to talk about his painting, this communication becomes an extension of the entire process. It can enhance and consummate the expression of an idea. But if forced or pursued without real desire on the part of the child, it is at best a waste of time, and it tends to lessen the intensity and positiveness of the total experience.

Since all children are different, the form and direction in which their creative potentialities should develop varies. Each, therefore, must be helped to find his own standards of performance and to appreciate his unique style as a facet of his total self. As he learns to use his faculties creatively, he becomes increasingly able to value his painting not only for the pleasure he derives from the process and his growing perception and because he can discern the quality that results from his use of color, line, and form, but also because he can recognize his work as an extension of himself.

Children and adults should appreciate the desirability of differences as well as similarities between human beings. This is not always natural. It needs to be cultivated, defended, and prized. The personal quality of a child's individual expression should be recognized and valued by the child, his parents, the group, the teacher, and all who see his work. Appreciation of one's own style and that of others helps everyone to realize that variety should be taken for granted and enjoyed:

"Each person experiences things in his own way and thus every distinguishable thing is seen and understood according to the approach of the beholder and not, as it might be, from its own point of view."*

---

*From *Meister Eckhart,* translated by Raymond B. Blakney (New York: Harper and Brothers, 1957).

The Paintings

The paintings in this collection were selected for their art quality or presence and as examples of individual expression. Many of them were chosen expressly because they are atypical — all too often the unusual painting is rejected in favor of more familiar, finished-looking, literal work that is actually less creative and original.

The order in which the paintings are arranged is designed to underscore the conviction that *chronological age* and *art age,* or developmental level, need not necessarily coincide, and that each individual's rate of growth may or may not be consistent with a set pattern. The variety of work in each age grouping supports this belief.

The selection shows the kind of painting that can be done in a classroom where the painting experience is a part of life rather than a separate discipline. The many techniques and media that can be offered are represented; the motivation for these paintings ranges from sources within the child's own autonomy to others either directly or indirectly related to the curriculum, including areas of interest such as science, social studies, language arts, and music.

Paintings by Five-year-olds

USING BIG BRUSHES
Mark Soma, age 5

Tempera on sterling manila paper

A wide selection of colors was made available to students by having many containers of paint on a common table. If a child wished, he could swap a color on his easel for a different choice. Children at this level usually paint in small groups at easels as well as on cardboard on the floor.

This painting was done at the beginning of the year. After general procedure and work habits for painting were fairly well established, some one- and one-and-a-half-inch utility brushes were added to the selection of brushes available. The novelty of the wide brush prompted Mark to use it to see how it "worked."

FILLING SPACE
Lehua Novit, age 5

Tempera on sterling manila paper

In this work some flat shapes and sponge prints were made with no discernible relation to each other. Then, the areas between them were filled in. There was some overpainting.

Lehua enjoyed using a new batch of clean colors and "filling space" with shapes, painting at her easel during a free period.

SHIP
Jon Liu, age 5

Tempera on sterling manila paper

The colors were chosen from a wide selection on the paint table. Flat areas of paint were combined with outlining and filling in. This was done during a free painting period when Jon could paint anything he wished, according to his own inner prompting. Ships and the sea are an integral part of his surroundings.

A DESIGN
Russell Heirakuji, age 5

Tempera on sterling manila paper

This painting incorporates areas that are outlined as well as shapes made without preliminary delineation, unpainted spaces and filled-in spaces. Designs of spots and lines and entire color fields are overpainted.

In his use of paint, Russell progressed quickly from manipulating the medium to creating and organizing forms. At a timely moment in the development of painting as a part of his daily program, he was helped to arrive at his own definition of a design and to begin to understand how designs can be made with lines, shapes, and colors. In this painting he expressed himself in designs using abstract shapes or symbols.

DESIGN
Kolu Kroll, age 5

Tempera on sterling manila paper

The paper was covered with outlined circular shapes of all sizes, and the shapes filled in with paint.

Several easels were set up for individual, free work, so Kolu worked on his own. Kolu selected and used a series of related forms to produce a strong design. It is interesting that he repeated the same colors and placed them to achieve balance in the design, and that he did not use *all* the colors available. He did not volunteer statements about his work, and no inquiry was made by the teacher.

TURKEY
Douglas Chang, age 5

Tempera on sterling manila paper

This painting was built up of flat color shapes that gradually progressed from forms representing the turkey to include the entire picture surface. There was very little overpainting. There had been some casual discussion about which was more appealing to the eye — the unpainted sheet of paper or the colors of the tempera. Some children began to add more color shapes to the space, while others elected to cover the entire surface with paint.

Seasonal songs, pictures, and stories underlined the anticipation of the Thanksgiving holiday. Douglas chose the turkey, the most exciting symbol of the event in the minds of the children, as the subject for his painting (compare the paintings on pages 42 and 51). He made it during a free time when some children worked at the easels, while others were involved in other activities.

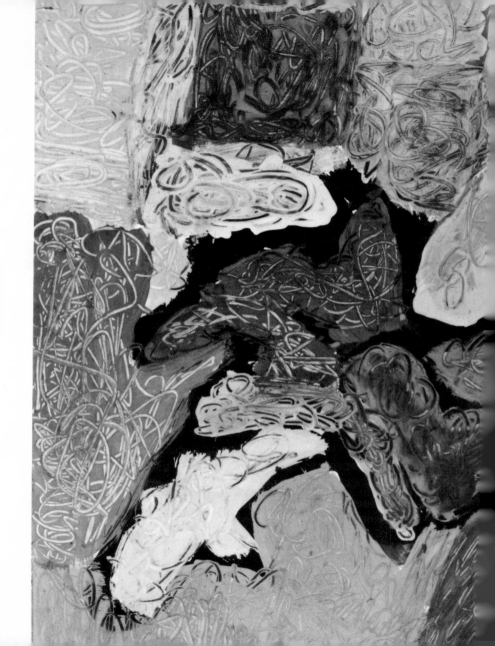

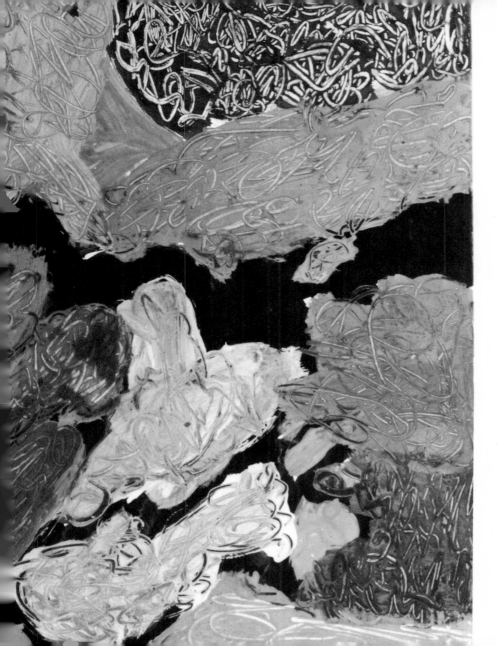

DESIGN
Cindy Caswell, age 5

Tempera and india ink on manila tag paper

The design of this scratch painting was made freely with tempera and india ink, and the resulting shapes and lines allowed to dry. A second coat of paint was applied to one area at a time and scratched into a texture with a small wooden stick. The scratching was done quickly, while the top layer of tempera was still wet and before the undercoat absorbed too much moisture. Some of the areas originally colored in india ink were left uncovered. This technique can be used with any medium that can be scratched to expose the painting surface or an undercoat. Other tools, such as the end of a brush, work too.

A preliminary discussion and experimentation with dark and light colors showed that a dark color must be covered with a lighter one, or vice versa, to ensure sufficient contrast when the scratching is done, and that the first coat of paint must be perfectly dry before overpainting if the scratched lines are to show up clearly.

Paintings by Six-year-olds

WHAT I DID ON THANKSGIVING
Randall Ishikawa, age 6

Oil crayon on sterling manila paper

In the first scene of this triple sequence, the figure of the boy was drawn in and then the background added. In the center, the bleachers assume primary importance: the less detailed figure was superimposed. In the last scene, the boy again assumes a dominant role, but was drawn, logically, *after* the bench he sits on. Randall continued to add color until his entire picture plane was filled in with kaleidoscopic shapes.

An actual experience provided the idea for the painting: it recalls what the child did on Thanksgiving Day — going to a football game and eating dinner. He dominates the sequence entirely because this story is about *his* day.

BISHOP MUSEUM
Zelda Nishimura, age 6

Tempera on sterling manila paper

Some areas of this painting were drawn in with tempera, others built up as planes of color. Overpainting was done on both damp and dry surfaces.

The Bishop Museum was built by Charles Reed Bishop as a memorial to his wife, Princess Bernice Pauahi, founder of The Kamehameha Schools. Grade One, in charge of the program that marks the yearly observance of Bishop's birthday, decided to paint a group of pictures illustrating some of the significant events of his life. One step in the development of the background for this activity was a trip to the Bishop Museum. In her painting, Zelda shows the facade of the massive building, which is built of hand-hewn volcanic rock.

GIANT SQUID
Hainani Keliikipi, age 6

Tempera and india ink on sterling manila paper

Here, the space divisions were painted in flat color, and the overpainting was done in ink and tempera.

This painting started out to be something else: it was well under way when the cardboard under it was jarred by a passing classmate and a jar containing some black ink was overturned in the middle of the paper. Hainani was distressed and wanted to abandon the painting, but the children who collected at the scene of the accident suggested that he could turn the large blob into something and immediately began to contribute ideas. Hainani's knowledge of the sea and the things that are found there gave him the idea of this big black sea creature. He spread the pool of ink into a form he liked and added additional detail to develop the new idea.

DIAMOND HEAD
Lee Ann Toguchi, age 6

Tempera on sterling manila paper

Linear design and areas of color were combined with some overpainting to achieve this design.

The interests developed and information gained by the class during a consideration of Honolulu in its role as the capital of Hawaii took shape in paintings, displays of illustrative materials, charts, and reports. Lee Ann gave a new and personal interpretation of Diamond Head, one of the most prominent physical features of the cityscape.

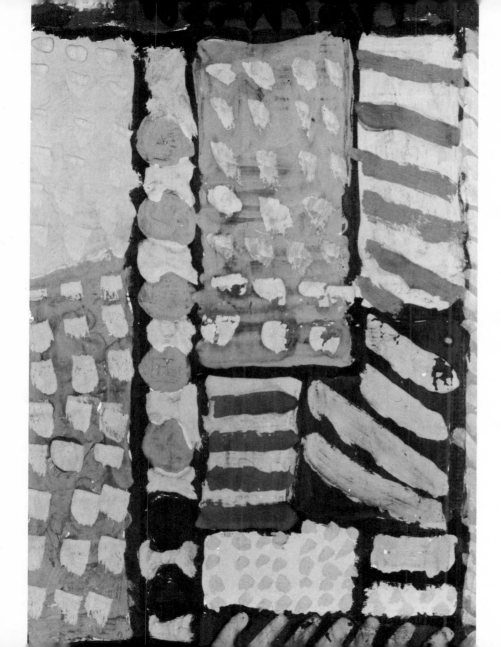

DESIGN ON NEWSPAPER
Norman Taira, age 6

Tempera and india ink on newspaper

Space divisions in newspaper layout were used as the basis for this design. The shapes defined in the basic design were colored in solidly. Some of the detail was added over these areas.

This was one of many excursions in the use of ordinary, easily available found materials. The work was done following a discussion in which the child was led to discover that the layout of a newspaper generally has a pattern made of straight lines resulting in geometric shapes, and that varying dark and light tonal qualities are created by the size and spacing of print.

FOLD-AND-BLOT DESIGN
Lilia Carpenter, age 6

Tempera on white manila paper

To make this fold-and-blot painting, the paper was folded vertically. Tempera was applied generously in the center fold and on one side of the paper to form lines, shapes, dribbles, and splashes. The paper was then folded together quickly and pressed firmly to transfer paint to the other side of the work surface. Blot patterns were made by forcing the larger amounts of paint into new shapes. Unfolding revealed the resulting "mirror" print. Additional color was applied until a satisfactory design or symmetrical motif resulted.

Fold-and-blot was introduced to the class as a type of printing-painting technique. Preliminary discussion and experimentation brought out the following facts. Paint must be applied heavily enough to be quite wet when the paper is folded; therefore it is best to work in small areas, blotting each before it dries. Overlapping produces rich new shades of color. Paint may cover all of the area, or unpainted areas may be left for contrast. The same paper may be folded alternately horizontally and vertically during the painting process to achieve more variety.

STRING DESIGN WITH TEMPERA
Amanda Machado, age 6

Tempera, ink, cotton yarn, and library paste on construction paper

The basic design elements of this work evolved from pasting scraps of yarn on the paper. Paint and ink were added.

Amanda had access to a "findings" box containing short lengths of various types of yarn. She was invited to see how many ways she could think of to use them on the paper surface, and this painting-collage was developed. Some of the other children looped, tied, or braided the yarn. These larger masses were exciting developments, but since they proved difficult to paste securely to the paper, they were kept for use in other projects.

DESIGN — i/t/a SYMBOLS
Stacy Plunkett, age 6

Tempera on Fadeless paper

The calligraphic lines of this work were painted on a black background, and some areas were filled in. The first-graders were learning to read and write by the i/t/a (Initial Teaching Alphabet) method. One day the beauty and design of the shapes of some symbols were discussed, and it was decided to use them in painting.

47

POLAR BEAR
Keoni Jardine, age 6

Tempera on sterling manila paper

This painting was done in large, simple color masses, with some overpainting.

A study of the Eskimo — his primitive culture and his adaptation for survival in a cold climate — constituted part of the social-studies program. As a result of a thorough saturation by books, films, and illustrations, Keoni was intrigued by the drama and exotic life of these people. This painting is one of many that grew out of his interest.

Although many colors were available, Keoni chose an unusually limited and appropriate palette. His choice (blue monochromatic) was not prompted by discussion or suggestion.

A CITY WITH BUILDINGS
Guy Kaulukukui, age 6

Tempera, india ink, and felt-tip ink marker on sterling manila paper

The space divisions (suggested by shapes of buildings) in this work were sponged on the paper: paint was applied to one side of the cut sponge with a brush and then spread with quick, even strokes. The pliability and absorbency of the sponge were increased by wetting and squeezing it before use. The linear design of the buildings was drawn on with ink; smaller details were added with an ink marker.

In a social-studies unit on the city, a bulletin board was posted with pictures showing different types of buildings. During a discussion of this exhibition, the children discovered that many designs and patterns result from the relationships of the buildings in a metropolitan area, and from windows, curtain walls, and other architectural or structural features. Some of the ideas that were discussed found expression in paintings, drawings, and wood design-constructions. Guy's idea of the city is one in which the component parts are massed together. The animals and people he uses in his painting are enclosed and subordinate.

TURKEY
Abraham Klein, age 6

Tempera and india ink on newspaper

This design was drawn with ink and a small brush, and parts of it were painted in.

One of the "seasonal" paintings preceding Thanksgiving, this was done on a day when the entire class opted to paint turkeys. Newspaper was introduced because its black-white-gray tone and pattern were compatible with the color and texture of the subject, and the children used varying amounts of color to enliven their work.

VALENTINE DESIGN WITH LEAVES
Abraham Klein, age 6

Tempera on sterling manila paper

As a result of overpainting, there are one to three layers of tempera in this painting. The surface tooling was achieved by using a stick to scratch through the top coat while it was still wet.

Looking for new material to exhibit in early February, the class naturally came up with the theme of Valentines. When they were asked, "What does Valentine's Day make you think of?" they led off with an almost unanimous response of "Valentines and hearts." The list was expanded to include things that give a Valentine "feeling," such as flowers, leaves, cupids, arrows, postmen, letters, lovebirds, and sweethearts. Some of these ideas were used by Abraham in his own design-interpretation.

EASTER EGG HUNT
Michael Soong, age 6

Tempera on sterling manila paper

In this painting-sponge print, the rabbits were painted in as lines, the eggs as shapes. The remaining areas were colored in with brush and sponge.

During the keen anticipation of Easter, many aspects of the season were brought out: its origin and meaning, the traditional observance of it, the plans made by the children for their vacation. Because of its special appeal to this age group, much of the interest revolved around the "Easter Bunny." The children gave their ideas about the role rabbits play in Easter, how big they are, how they move, how they look, and what they do. The Kindergarten rabbits were brought to the classroom, and stories and poems were read. This rich well of knowledge and feeling was the source of Michael's expression in his painting.

A DESIGN ABOUT THE CITY
Carla Aiwohi, age 6

Tempera and india ink on sterling manila paper

Tempera was applied to a damp sponge with a large brush, and the painting was executed with a printing technique plus sponged-on circles and strokes. In some parts of the design several colors were used on the sponge at once. Ink lines were added with a brush.

This is one of several painting and design experiences that grew out of a discussion of the concept of the city. (Compare the painting on page 49.) A response to the patterns that occur in individual structures and in the massing of large and small buildings prompted Carla to do her very free painting.

LEI DAY — FLOWERS EVERYWHERE
Hainani Keliikipi, age 6

Tempera on sterling manila paper

In this painting the large flower masses were made first. This was followed by overpainting in their centers and in other sections of the picture.

In the Hawaiian tradition, May Day is celebrated with many special events. All the children from Kindergarten through Grade Six participate in a pageant, which includes songs, music, dances, and ancient chants. This painting was suggested by a phrase from one of the songs: "garlands of flowers everywhere."

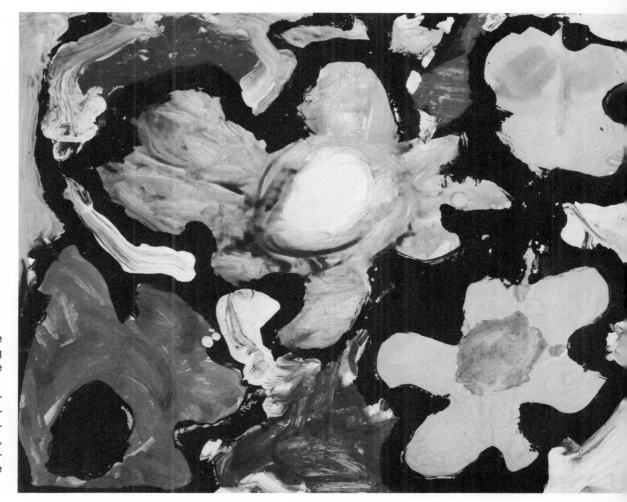

PAINTING TO MUSIC
Linda Hutchins, age 6

Tempera on white drawing paper

A damp sponge, to which paint was applied with a brush, was used to make this work. At times, several colors were painted on the sponge in stripes. Some overpainting was used.

The experience of painting to music was preceded by an interchange of ideas about how different things might move in water, still air, or a gusty wind and how the body is prompted to respond in different ways to music of varying rhythms. Acting out how to melt like wax, grow like a plant, wilt, be boneless or charged with electricity also served to limber up mind and body prior to the actual process of painting.

In order to keep the mechanics simple so that they would interfere as little as possible with the translation of sound to paper, and to keep the work large and free, in this initial experience only one technique — sponge painting — was used. At other times additional media are available and used singly or in combination, depending upon the child and the situation (compare the paintings on pages 68, 86, 87, bottom and 96, top).

Linda first assembled all the materials necessary to begin painting with one color. When she was settled comfortably, the music was played. She listened and absorbed the rhythm and mood until she felt that she was one with the music, then began her painting. New colors and clean sponges were quietly obtained as needed.

FIRST EXPERIENCE WITH WATERCOLOR
Herbert Henriques, age 6

Watercolor on white drawing paper

One or two brushfuls of water were applied to all pans of color in the watercolor box for preliminary softening. The brush, large enough to hold generous amounts of color, was washed out between color changes and partially dried on a small, squeezed-out sponge.

Watercolor was introduced as an extension of the painting experience; some children could identify the box of colors when they saw it. There was some discussion of the name of the medium, the reason for its name, how it was made, how it could be used, and its qualities as compared with other media the children had used.

A brief demonstration of how to assemble the items needed in preparation for painting and how to load the brush with color and wash it between color changes gave the children an understanding of the reason for keeping the colors in the box separate and clean. They were encouraged to use the medium freely and to see what they could do with it.

THE POLICEMAN
Harding Parrilla, Jr., age 6

Tempera on sterling manila paper

This was painted broadly with rather large brushes. Some overpainting and color-mixing on the painting surface resulted in blended colors.

The painting developed from and was the culmination of a study of people who serve the community — who they are and how they help. Stories, films, and excursions added new ideas to a list of professions the children already knew. For his painting, Harding chose the policeman as a figure he admired and would like to become. When his painting was posted, it had a printed caption that had been dictated by Harding, summing up what he had learned about the subject.

Paintings by Seven-year-olds

FIGURE IN A CIRCLE
James Miura, Jr., age 7

Tempera and india ink on screen milling paper

Lines were drawn in ink, most of the areas in the design painted with tempera, and the lines redefined. Drybrush texture designs were done in one unpainted area and then added to most of the painted surfaces.

Large circles of paper were presented to the class as a change from the usual rectangular painting paper. James was asked to visualize what happens to shapes when they are forced to conform to circular boundaries. This evoked the recollection of being curled up in a culvert pipe on the playground and in a swing made from a rubber tire. James made doodles and sketches on small circles of scrap paper to help him determine how he could adapt his idea to the space. Barrels, baskets, balloons, and drums were mentioned as other places where flexible objects would have to adapt themselves to fit inside a circular perimeter. The list was extended to include things suggested by or compatible with circular containers, such as fish, snakes, vines, water, and spaghetti.

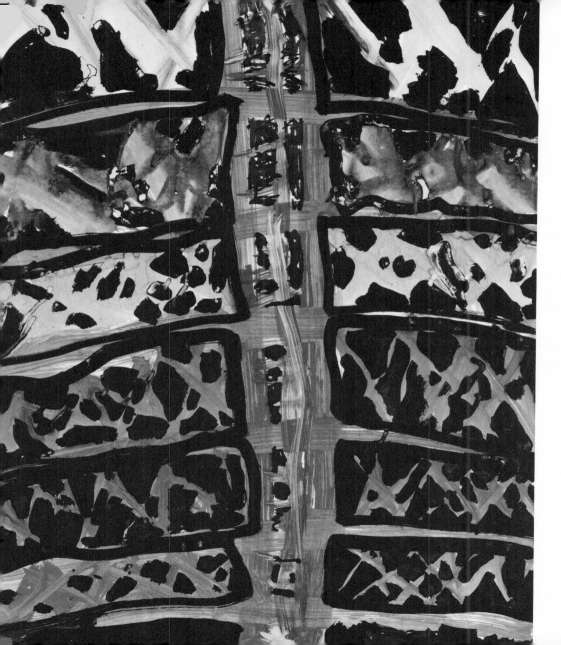

LEAF EATEN BY CATERPILLAR, CLOSE-UP
Paul Lucas, age 7

Tempera and felt-tip ink marker on sterling manila paper

For this work a linear color design was done in tempera and the spaces were filled in with ink marker.

The children searched within the classroom to find something *very small* that would make an interesting painting if it were greatly enlarged. Paintings were inspired by such items as a staple gun, paper clips, a small flower, and, in this case, a single leaf eaten by a caterpillar: Paul magnified the leaf skeleton to create a design that is architectural in character.

"BEETLE" CLOWN
Mara Gandia, age 7

Tempera on sterling manila paper

This painting was planned as a linear design and filled in with paints varying in consistency from a thin, transparent wash to a creamy, opaque paste.

Mara's anticipation of a circus which was coming to town was intensified by advertisements, illustrations, discussions, and plans to attend. She combined the circus theme with another of her interests to create her version of a clown.

VALENTINE IDEAS
Wallace Wong, age 7

Tempera and felt-tip ink marker on sterling manila paper

Tempera was applied with a brush to the damp sponge and painted on the paper in long strokes to produce the basic pattern. The ink-marker drawing was added over the dry paint.

Preliminary to the painting session, the children were asked why they thought Valentines were exchanged. They came to the conclusion that Valentines are given to people who are liked very much or loved. Wallace thought of all the things he personally associated with affection and used some of them in this design (compare the painting on page 50).

SPACE MAN
Alvin Baptista, age 7

Chalk and india ink on white manila paper

This design was drawn first with india ink. Then, one at a time, various areas were wet with a brush and water, and chalk was applied heavily to the surface. The chalk dissolved, forming color and texture effects unlike those of dry chalk. Other ink lines were drawn after the chalk was used, and there was some re-wetting and overpainting with chalk.

The painting was done following a general discussion that stemmed from the question, "What would you like to be when you grow up?" Alvin chose the astronaut, who, because of contemporary emphasis on man's exploration and conquest of space, joins the group of professions that stimulate the imagination of child and adult alike.

DESIGN — EXPERIMENTING WITH PAINT
Kent Kam, age 7

Tempera on sterling manila paper

As soon as the spiral design was painted in tempera, the paper was clipped to a cardboard work board and propped up vertically. Some very thin blue paint was applied by flicking it with the fingers. Dripping and sprinkling were tried but did not have sufficient force to be effective.

The idea for this work originated when several paintings posted outside the classroom were sprinkled by a blowing shower of rain. The colors ran, making an interesting effect, but the effect did not contribute anything to the paintings, which had definite subject matter. It was decided that the technique might work better with abstract motifs.

During the process of experimenting, first with water and then with thin color, Kent found that he got better results if the color was flicked on while the ground coat was still quite damp.

ABORIGINE DESIGN
Jeri Baker, age 7

Tempera wash, india ink, and crayon on sterling manila paper

A drawing, approximating a small preliminary sketch, was made in ink on sterling manila. The paper was wet on the back and crumpled, without twisting, in two directions — from side to side and from top to bottom. It was then smoothed out gently, and tempera wash was applied with a sponge. Some areas were crayoned in, and some lines redone with black crayon. Most students did not cover all of the paper, but Jeri's color is especially rich because she colored the entire surface.

This mixed-media painting was done as a result of a social-studies unit on the Aborigine tribes of Australia, for which a collection of handsome reproductions of bark paintings was obtained from a museum. It led to a discussion of materials, techniques, colors, and subjects used by these primitive people and prompted the class to try making their own interpretations of this method of painting (compare the painting on page 75).

61

A RAINY DAY
Kaui Kapele III, age 7

Tempera on sterling manila paper

This was painted with a very full brush on a humid day, so the paint dried very slowly. Some rather manipulative handling of paint was combined with quite a bit of over-painting and mixing on the painting surface.

The motivation for the work was a cessation of the trade winds, followed by a blustery rainstorm, which caused the flooding of many streets, fallen trees, stalled cars, power failures, school-bus delays, and other dramatic incidents. Kaui was full of the excitement and joined his classmates in relating some of his experiences. Here he expressed the mood of the rainy day on which it was done.

BOY WITH GUITAR
Albert Kam, age 7

Tempera on white drawing paper

This painting was executed broadly with large, rather abstract shapes, some details accented with line.

Vocal and instrumental music play an integral, vital role in the life of the Hawaiian child, both in school and at home. Many paintings are inspired by the children's own experiences with instruments they have seen or can play. Although this particular painting followed a demonstration by several members of the Honolulu Symphony Orchestra, the child's perception and interpretation are in terms of the music he knows best.

ONE OF THE THREE KINGS
Mark Furtado, age 7

Chalk and crayon on construction paper

This drawing was done in crayon on gray construction paper. It was colored with chalk, which was applied heavily, rubbed into the paper, and fixed with plastic spray. (Only those paintings that go out on exhibit are sprayed. For general use, the rubbing is sufficient to prevent smearing.)

Mark chose to paint one of the Wise Men after a pre-Christmas review of the story of the birth of Jesus, when many aspects of the subject, including persons and scenes, were enumerated. He made a preliminary sketch in crayon on scrap paper to decide what he wanted to include in his picture.

STRING PAINTING
Paul Lucas, age 7

India ink and cotton yarn on Fadeless paper

This painting was made with a length of string approximately sixteen to twenty inches long. All except a few inches of "handle" was dipped in a little ink in a shallow can. The saturated string was laid on non-absorbent paper, and the design achieved by pulling and trailing it over and dropping it on the surface.

Painting with string was introduced as an excursion and diversion — this is one way of using techniques to stimulate children's imagination, lend variety to their painting experiences, and add to their art vocabulary and skills.

Paul skipped the purely manipulative stage: all of his paintings showed deliberate planning and control. This particular work, done on a large sheet of paper, was one of several done during the art period.

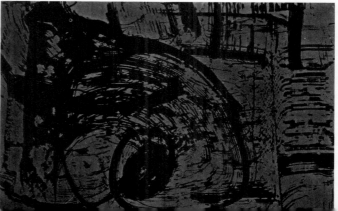

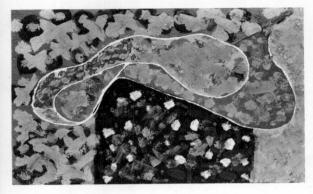

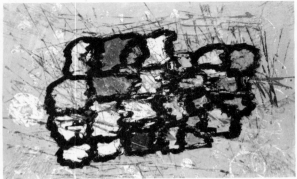

STRING DESIGN
Stephen Kauka, age 7

Tempera, cotton yarn, and liquid paste on kranila tag paper

Yarn was dipped in liquid paste, and the excess paste squeezed out by running the yarn through the fingers. It was pressed firmly on the paper. Then the surface was painted. When the paint was quite dry, the string was pulled off, leaving an unpainted line.

This string-resist painting began as a challenge to invention. Stephen was given a length of yarn to see how many variations he could make using one continuous line within a given space. He experimented with moving the yarn around on the paper background. When he got an arrangement that he liked, he pasted it down. He painted in the shapes defined by the line and further enriched them by overpainting with brush and sponge.

DESIGN WITH STICK PRINTING
Colleen Ann Char, age 7

Tempera on white drawing paper

The entire sheet of paper was painted in one color, then other colors and black lines were added. Patterns were stamped over the basic design with spools, paper tubes, sticks, and other objects that had been painted with the medium.

The painting was made during one of a series of explorations in the uses of tempera. Colleen was the only member of the class to use the process described. Such variations in the use of media challenge children's ability to imagine and to innovate and also increase their skill in the control of tools and materials.

COLLAGE WITH PAINT
Danton Naone, age 7

Tempera, cloth scraps, buttons, india ink, paste, Duco Cement, and corrugated paper on cardboard

The materials for this collage, chosen from separate boxes set out for easy access, were pasted on lightweight gray cardboard with library paste (except for the buttons, which were glued on with Duco Cement). Danton decided to add india ink and tempera to his collage after he had finished assembling and pasting it.

The idea of making collages originated when one of the boys brought in a box of cloth scraps in vibrant solid colors. The pieces, which came from a garment factory, were too small for sewing, but the shapes were interesting, and it was decided that they would make good designs. Other supplies and findings, including shop "ends" of gray cardboard, yarn scraps, small pieces of corrugated cardboard, buttons, and paper trimmings, were collected. There was a discussion about whether it was better to begin with small shapes or large ones and how to get a good bond between cloth and paper.

Paintings by Eight-year-olds

CANOE
Marcus Rosehill, age 8

Tempera on sterling manila paper

Canoe, figures, and fish were superimposed on the flat background areas of this painting.

During a study of transportation, the class listed the methods used by man to move himself and his goods from one place to another: feet, skateboards, wheeled vehicles, and water and air transport were included. Dugout canoes, used both in Old Hawaii and today, interested Marcus. His X-ray view shows that he remembers not only seeing such canoes but having been in one.

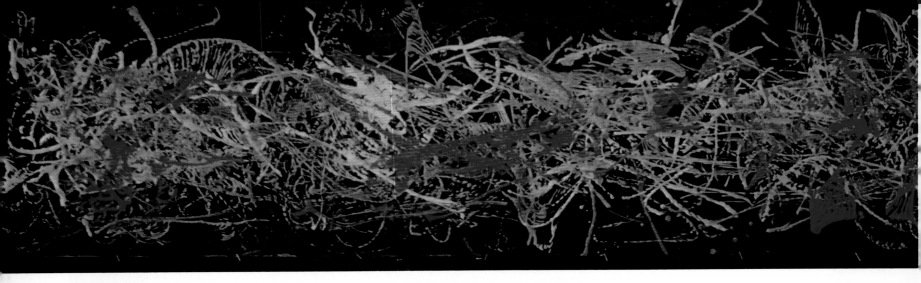

STRING DESIGN (detail)
Group work, ages 8-9

Tempera and cotton yarn on Fadeless paper

Lengths of rug yarn, eighteen to twenty-four inches long,
were dipped in a shallow container of tempera, and the
pattern was produced by dragging, trailing, and manipulating the string in other ways on the surface.
   During a period when most of the class had been
string-painting, a couple of children finished their individual experiments earlier than their classmates. They
thought it would be fun to work together. A length of
paper was cut to fit one of the bulletin boards in the
room. The two students began to work on this and were
soon joined by other children, until there were eight or so
involved in the painting.

BUFFALO ROUND-UP (detail)
Group work (twenty-five children), ages 8-9

Tempera and india ink on 48-inch-wide sterling manila
roll paper

Most of the mural was done directly in painted shapes.
Some outlines were made as preliminary drawing, and
some were added later as accents.
   The idea of doing a mural came during the culmination
of a study of the Indians of the American Southwest. The
buffalo round-up was an event in the lives of these inhab-
itants of desert country that had great appeal to the class.
Each child added some element to the central theme:
some contributed animals and people involved in the
round-up itself, while others set the scene with cactus,
tumbleweed, and other background features.

LINE RHYTHMS DONE TO MUSIC
Grayling Achiu, age 8

Tempera wash, crayon, and india ink on white manila paper

The crayon lines of this resist painting were drawn to music; the color was built up in tempera washes applied with a small sponge. Additions in crayon and ink were made later.

During a free dialogue between teacher and class, the children imagined and drew "in the air" patterns created by moving objects, and they described some of the effects that can be created by varying lines and shapes. A selection of illustrations that gave the *effect* of motion was shown with the opaque projector: the stroboscopic swirls of dancers' skirts, fireworks, flames, and the warped skeletons of wrecked buildings.

After each child got all his materials ready, a few moments of quiet concentration on the music prefaced the actual beginning of the painting or drawing. Some chose to begin directly with crayon, ink, or paint, while others preferred drawing on sketch paper at their seats until they achieved a rhythmic effect they felt was right.

TWO MEN TALKING
David Yamamoto, age 8

Tempera on white drawing paper

This was painted and overprinted. There are three layers of paint in some of printed areas.

The idea for this painting came from a discussion about what was the most important thing in the world to the children or to any person. The conclusions reached were that, in most instances, the most important thing to man was *himself;* that man belonged to the category of people (as opposed to birds, fish, insects); that pictures with people in them were interesting to other people; and that the class liked to watch people of all kinds doing things.

MOON RISING OVER THE PALI
George Kahumoku, age 8

Tempera on white drawing paper

Here, flatly painted spaces serve as background (sea, land, sky) for overpainted details.

A discussion and study of Oahu, the island where Honolulu is located, was the basis of this work. The children described places and scenes they knew about, and George's idea was translated into this very individual statement. The painting was exhibited with others done by the class to summarize their experiences and knowledge.

MEDIEVAL CHURCH
Mark Duvauchelle, age 8

Watercolor and india ink on white drawing paper

The drawing was done partially in ink; additional drawing and colors were added in watercolor.

A medieval wood carving of a madonna and child, an intricate model of a Gothic chapel, and some small examples of stained glass were brought to the classroom from a school display case housing an early-December exhibition of objects from an art museum's lending collection. The objects were examined carefully and discussed, and their influence was felt in some of the paintings that followed.

Mark's interpretation took the form of an almost abstract composition incorporating the chapel, its stained glass windows (both in idea and style), and the madonna (center arch). Although the models were in front of Mark during the entire work period, the painting is a translation of them into his own terms.

MOON AND CLOUDS
Jo Ann Melemai, age 8

Tempera on white drawing paper

The tempera used to paint this contained a lot of water but was still almost opaque in places when applied to the paper.

Jo Ann did her painting during a free period, with no discussion of motivation. It is probably a recollection of the dramatic sight of the moon, visibly enlarged by atmospheric conditions, as it rises behind a series of moving clouds. The ridge of mountains forming the backbone of the island where she lives is usually capped by massed clouds that break up and evaporate as the wind pushes them toward the ocean.

STATUE OF BUDDHA
Barbara Antolin, age 8

Tempera on white drawing paper

In this painting some of the flat background area was overpainted with a sponge.

Barbara, an inhabitant of a city where numerous temples and churches exist in close harmony, visited a museum where statues from many faiths are exhibited. She was particularly impressed by a statue of Buddha. In her painting she divorces the image from its actual appearance and captures the essence of the form as she felt it.

FIRE IN VOLCANO
Brant Crabbe, age 8

Tempera on sterling manila paper

Thin tempera was applied in a manner suggested by the subject matter of this painting.

When a volcano on the island of Hawaii is active, it creates quite a bit of excitement. Pele, the goddess of the volcano, is well known to all residents of the Hawaiian chain. During an eruption the display of fountains of molten lava and flame is particularly effective at night, as Brant's painting illustrates. Evidence of his previous experiences of painting to music is seen in this free translation of his concept into lines and shapes characteristic of the subject.

ABORIGINES OF AUSTRALIA
Martha Farrar, age 8

Tempera on sterling manila paper

Outlined shapes that are filled in were alternated with mass-shapes that are outlined. Some overpainting was used, in addition to scratching.

During a study of the Australian Aborigines, all the children made sketches of what they thought was an interesting aspect of life in this primitive culture. Most of the sketches were made into paintings (see, for example, pages 61 and 75) which, with explanatory captions, were posted in the classroom. Martha, whose own Hawaiian tradition is closely related to the dance, decided to depict this activity.

MARY WITH VEIL
Wesley Kitaoka, age 8

Cold-water dye and india ink on screen milling paper

This work originated as a cartoon for a resist painting on cloth. The india-ink drawing served as a guide in the application of crayon to the cloth. After the crayoning was completed, the screen milling paper was kept as a backing during the application of the dyes. Although the paper absorbed some of the excess dye, additional color was needed, so more dyes were applied to complete the painting. The artistic quality of the inked guidelines, the pleasing texture of the gray paper, and the blotted colors of the dyes absorbed by the paper led Wesley to see the cartoon as a painting in itself.

IN THE PARK
Donna Lee Ah Sam, age 8

Crayon, cold-water dye, india ink, screen milling paper, and cloth

A sketch was drawn lightly with white chalk on screen milling paper (the same size as the cloth to be used) to allow for changing and adapting the idea to suit the space. The final drawing was done with india ink and a small brush (crayon may be used). The cloth was pinned over the drawing, and crayon lines were applied to both sides of the cloth. Cold-water dye was painted on with a large soft brush, and the cloth was left pinned to the paper to dry.

The children in this class had done resist painting on paper in Kindergarten and in Grades One and Two. In Grade Three, the experience was extended to working on cloth with a similar process. They brought in old sheets, and the usable portions were torn into rectangles averaging eighteen by twenty-four inches in size. The technique of resist painting was reviewed. Since the dye to be used would bleed quite a bit, it was decided that most of the areas of the designs should be made with closed lines, and the crayon applied heavily to separate the color areas. The character of the technique is such that most ideas are necessarily translated in terms of linear design, but the children were free to choose any subject. Preliminary sketches in pencil or crayon were made to determine subject and design.

SHIPS AT THE PIER (HONOLULU HARBOR)
Patrick Cullen, age 8

PALM TREE
Nazha Miranda, age 8

COLLAGE WITH CIRCLE
Kanani Tirrell, age 8

Oil crayon, glazed paper, rug yarn, and library paste on construction paper

For this collage, glazed paper was cut and pasted on construction paper, oil crayon added on the background, and the work edged with yarn. To extend experiments combining paper and various painting media, the design problem required the use of a limited number of small sheets of paper — one, two, or three, as the child chose. All the sheets had to be used. The design could be non-objective or it could express an idea.

For her design, Kanani cut and expanded two sheets, arranging them so each of the two colors covered half the picture plane. Her crayon addition unified the composition and enriched the pattern.

Tempera and india ink on sterling manila paper

This painting was done in broad, flat planes. The bold black outlines were added when the surface was completely dry.

Honolulu is called the Crossroads of the Pacific. The harbor — Aloha Tower, a battery of piers, and many kinds of ships and smaller craft — can be seen from the classroom *lanai* (porch) where the children frequently work in art and other activities. One section of the panorama prompted this work.

Crayon, cold-water dye, india ink, screen milling paper, chalk, and cloth.

A preliminary drawing was done in chalk on paper until satisfactory spacing was achieved. It was then inked in and covered with cloth, which was pinned to the backing paper. The outlines of the design showed through the cloth and were crayoned in heavily. The dye was applied with large, soft brushes.

The introduction of dye, a totally new medium to the children, and the use of cloth stimulated many ideas for the extension of their experience with resist painting (compare the painting on page 72, top). This child's choice of subject matter was derived from the natural surroundings, palm trees being one of the most typical features of the landscape.

73

THREE CATS
Elizabeth Bright, age 8

Chalk and crayon on white drawing paper

Chalk and crayon were combined in this painting. There was some overlapping of colors and of the media. A small amount of the surface was scratched.

Animals are next in importance to people (see the painting on page 69, left) in the child's lexicon of living things, and this picture was prompted by Elizabeth's choice of her favorite animal. She was encouraged to tell as much as possible about the animal — where he lived, what he was doing, when the event of her painting occurred (day or night), and what the weather was like.

ABORIGINE WITH BIRDS
Stephanie Souza, age 8

Crayon and india ink on natural kraft paper

The design was drawn on the paper with india ink and left to dry completely. The paper was then wet on the back with a sponge and crumpled, but not twisted, until a satisfactory texture resulted. Areas were colored in wax crayon, and some ink lines were re-covered with black crayon. (The children planned to collect and use colored earth in place of crayon in a future project.)

During a study of the primitive culture of the Australian Aborigines, one of the classroom teachers got a collection of wonderful color prints showing pictures of the people, their homes, some of the tools they use, and other aspects of their life, including bark paintings. Sketches were made by each child to show what he would paint if he were an aborigine making a bark painting. The crumpled paper (from a common brown paper bag) was the most easily available material for approximating the bark surface.

75

FIREWORKS
Richard Furtado, age 8

Tempera and ink on sterling manila paper

The lines in the center of this design were painted with a brush. In other areas paint was dripped, "splatted," and applied with the fingers — many of the round spots were made by dipping the fingers in a drop of paint already on the paper and printing with them.

The oriental tradition of fireworks for special occasions is still evident in Hawaii. Strings of firecrackers are set off at building dedications, anniversaries, birthdays, and other important events. The New Year is greeted with a blaze of light and a fury of sound. This painting is one child's idea of a sky full of exploding fireworks. As he painted it, he accompanied himself with appropriate verbalization and sound effects.

Paintings by Nine-year-olds

SHAKING THE NET
Bryan Ahue, age 9

Water and india ink on cream manila paper

The figures and net were drawn with ink; then watercolor was used freely to suggest the background.

Beginning in Kindergarten, Hawaiian language, music, and culture are a part of the school program at Kamehameha. In Grade Four there is special emphasis on Hawaiiana, and much of the children's work in art, crafts, music, language, and dance is inspired by this concentrated study. As a culmination of it, the children stage a brief enactment of the ancient ceremony of *Makahiki.* This annual thanksgiving was observed to thank the gods for the good year past and as a prayer for the year to come. During the ceremony, vegetable foods are laid in a net which is lifted and shaken: if the food falls through, it forecasts a good harvest.

Bryan's intent was to show the children who played this role in the pageant. His interpretation captures the mood and essence of the precise moment when the ancient command is chanted in Hawaiian: "Shake down the god's food. Scatter it, oh heaven . . . life to the land!"

HAWAIIAN MONARCHS:
KALAKAUA (left) and KAMEHAMEHA IV
Group work (three or four children), ages 9-10

Tempera on brown kraft paper

These compositions were drawn lightly in chalk before painting began. Parts of the designs as well as details were done by overpainting.

The paintings, two of eight three- by six-foot portraits of Hawaiian monarchs, were planned and executed by volunteers for an annual Lei Day program. Each of the children who participated made a preliminary sketch based on photographs, illustrations, and color slides of models in the museum.

UNUSUAL ANIMAL
Hope Ah Loo, age 9

Tempera and ink on sterling manila paper

This painting was built up with flat color areas, and much decorative design was added by overpainting in ink and tempera.

During a discussion intended to encourage innovative thinking, it was brought out that each individual is the "boss" of his own picture. Hope learned that neither color nor form need be real, because in paint on paper she could express her idea any way *she* chose. In the painting that followed, she made a recognizable form and then proceeded to elaborate it into this fanciful design.

WORKING IN RICE PADDY
Thyzra Ann Keaweehu, age 9

Tempera on screen milling paper

Built-up shapes, filled-in areas, and overpaint-ing were combined in this work.

A committee chose the subject of the pro-duction and distribution of food for study. They did research on the importance of rice in countries where it is the staple food and in-vestigated methods of cultivation, harvesting, and marketing. (They also prepared rice sever-al ways and served it to the class as a part of their report.) Thyzra made this painting as a part of her individual presentation on cultiva-tion.

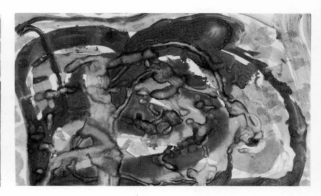

SPACE
Faith Kamaka, age 9

Tempera on manila tag paper

This was painted freely on lightweight paper. The white drip and spatter work on the surface was done to achieve a special effect of vibrant movement.

After a study of space, planets, the solar system, and galaxies, Faith had a thorough background in the subject matter. In this painting she tried to express *motion* in space with line, color, and shape.

FANTASY
Kim Crowell, age 9

Tempera on screen milling paper

The creature in the center was outlined and filled in; then the other forms were built up and overpainted.

This work followed a brainstorming session set off by the use of the word *fantasy* and a discussion of its definition. It was concluded that in the context of painting, fantasies could take the form of imaginary beings and objects in an unreal relationship or setting. Kim structured her painting around the main, recumbent creature, adding other forms as she worked into the rest of the painting field.

PAINTING TO MUSIC
Karen Chai, age 9

Tempera on white drawing paper

This painting was done with a sponge dipped in a small amount of tempera. Additional paint and some clear water were dripped on.

After a consideration of music and its power to stimulate the imagination and prompt expression through responding body movements, Karen listened to a selection. By fusing her emotional response with physical movement, she achieved this visualization in line, shape, and color.

Stephanie S.

CLASSMATE
Edward Kameenui, age 9

Watercolor, india ink, and crayon on white drawing paper

The drawing was done in india ink and colored with crayon and watercolor.

This was an exercise in drawing from a model, motivated by Edward's desire to handle figures with more facility. He was given the choice of making a study of the head, a three-quarter figure, or the entire body, and it could be related to the actual background or transposed to any surroundings he desired. He painted this portrait directly, with no preliminary sketching or blocking in.

DAY AND NIGHT
Stephanie Souza, age 9

Watercolor crayon on white drawing paper

This painting was created by wetting the paper with a sponge, one area at a time, and coloring it with the broad side of the crayon. Additional water was added for overpainting.

Mountains and ocean are prominent parts of the view from many places on the island where Stephanie lives. Here she used the mountain as the setting for her conception of the delineation between day and night.

SHEPHERD KEEPING WATCH OVER FLOCK
Donalei Ho, age 9

Oil crayon, felt-tip ink marker, colored tissue paper, and liquid starch on manila tag paper

The drawing in this collage was done freehand with an ink marker on the working surface. Starch was painted on the areas to be covered with tissue paper, and the tissue was laid in place and painted over with another coat of starch. When the collage was quite dry, ink marker was used to accent some of the lines, and oil crayon was applied to add pattern and color. Overlapping tissue also created varying color intensity and mixed shades.

Before Christmas, several children planned a series of illustrations built around the Nativity story from the Bible (compare the painting on page 63, top). Each child made preliminary sketches to clarify his idea and then proceeded to develop it, using the media in common with the rest of the group, but working individually.

TIKI ON KAPA
Gilbert Tam, age 9

Tempera, chalk, and india ink on sterling manila roll paper

The design was drawn first in chalk, then in ink. When the ink was completely dry, the paper was wet on both sides with a sponge, "gathered" together, and squeezed without twisting. After the process of squeezing was repeated in the opposite direction, the paper was opened gently and spread smooth while still damp.

Visits to the Bishop Museum gave Gilbert a knowledge of many aspects of life in ancient Hawaii. He saw dioramas using life-sized human casts, models of *heiaus* (temples), and an authentically constructed thatched house. He learned about the arts and crafts of the people — their musical instruments, stone tools, bone fishhooks, surfboards, outrigger canoes, *kapa* (bark cloth), and *tikis* (carved wooden gods). In this painting he chose to depict a *tiki,* and he crumpled the paper to achieve a color and texture similar to that of *kapa* (compare the procedure used to make the paintings on pages 61 and 75). For the background pattern he used some of the basic line motifs found in authentic *kapas.*

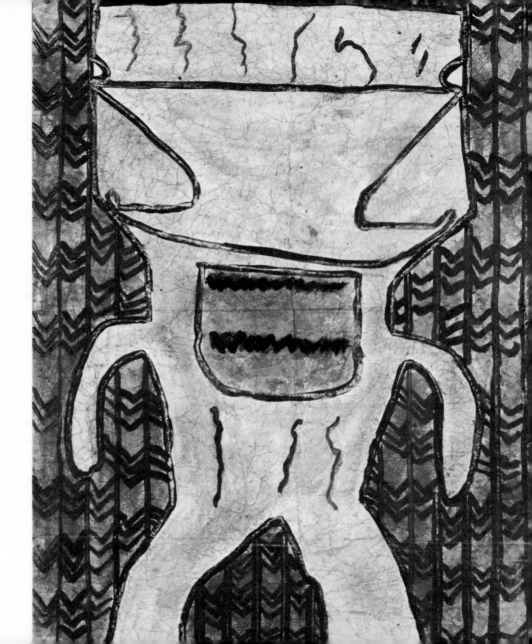

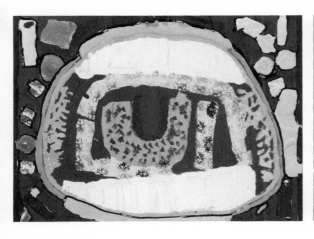

AN OPEN MOUTH
Karen Lum, age 9

Tempera on sterling manila paper

This work was executed in flat areas with some overpainting and sponge printing.

Immediately following a discussion about what some of the ideas most often seen in paintings are, a brainstorming session was held. It was designed to stretch the children's imagination to seek out and invent subjects that they had never seen in a painting or that they thought unlikely to be seen. This painting was Karen's response to the stimulus created by the interchange of ideas with her classmates.

SLAVE WORKING ON PLANTATION
Jo-Anne Hugo, age 9

Tempera on sterling manila paper

Painting of areas and shapes, outlining, color-mixing on the surface, and overpainting were combined to create this work.

During a study of food (compare the painting on page 80), the class discussed early methods of production and present-day techniques. This painting was done by one member of a committee that elected to study the historical role of agricultural labor in the United States and was used to illustrate the joint report of the group.

MY SISTER AND I SLEEP IN BUNK BEDS
Francine Peneku, age 9

Tempera and felt-tip ink marker on white drawing paper

Most of this painting was done in flat areas laid in without preliminary outlines. Some parts of the picture, including the arms, the leaves on the tree, and the top of the stool, were drawn in with tempera or marker. Additional details and outlining were also done with marker.

Francine constantly made sketches to record things that she saw, did, or thought. Many of her ideas, such as this one taken from actual experience, were translated into paint.

Paintings by Ten-year-olds

JITTERBUGS DANCING
Noel Smith, age 10

Tempera on used construction paper

The basic pattern of movement in mass and line was accented by additional lines to establish mood and tempo.

This painting stemmed from Noel's individual response to hearing rock-and-roll music, watching other dancers, and beginning to participate himself.

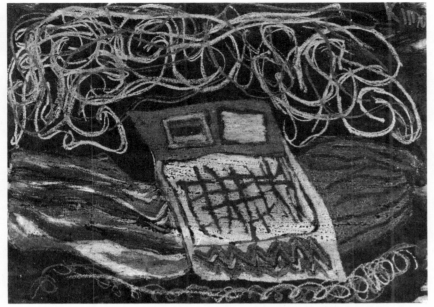

PAINTING TO MUSIC, HALLOWEEN
Kimo Miller, age 10

Tempera and oil crayon on screen milling paper

The drawing in crayon was covered with a tempera wash to make this resist painting.

In this direct response to music, Kimo employed patterns evoked by the mood of the selection heard ("Hall of the Mountain King," *Peer Gynt Suite*). He did the work when Halloween was imminent, and there had been some discussion of ideas that were in keeping with the spirit of the season. The title and theme of the record and discussion of the music were deliberately omitted before the painting experience so that the children would not be influenced by anyone else's interpretation.

MUSIC — CITY AND RIVERS
Avis Ing, age 10

Tempera on white drawing paper

This was executed freely with brush and sponges and overpainted while wet.

Avis painted this design as her response to "The Rivers," a selection from a record titled *New York, New York*. She did not know the name of the album or the excerpt played; nevertheless, she captured the feeling of the masses of buildings and the curving, flowing lines of the rivers.

SEASHORE
David Bray, age 10

Tempera on manila tag paper

This was painted directly, with no preliminary sketching. The color was mixed in the palette (an egg-tray) and on the painting surface.

The work was one of a series of painting experiments done during a study of motion and mood and how they can be expressed by line, color, and shape. The painting took shape during the process rather than being predetermined: as the child painted, the color and design suggested the subject-theme, which he developed into a finished painting.

TWO CHIEFS BRING GIFTS TO AN ALII
Annette Kama, age 10

Tempera on white drawing paper

Some shapes in this painting were outlined and filled in with color; others were painted as color areas. There was much overpainting and mixing on the surface. Linear accents were added to define the important forms.

Having Hawaiian ancestry and attending a school close to a museum devoted to the Polynesian cultures, Annette naturally developed an interest in the ancient Hawaiian people. She was familiar with their history as it was handed down in old chants and legends and recorded by the earliest visitors to the islands. Her concentration on the subject led to the painting of this scene — her conception of the birth of an *alii* (chief or king). Annette connected the idea with a similar event — the Nativity of the Bible.

DESIGN WITH PAINT AND FINDINGS
William Kuhns, age 10

Tempera, crayon, chalk, glazed paper, magazine clippings, cloth, and library paste on Fadeless paper

The basic design of this collage was achieved by fixing findings to the paper background with paste. The thick paste enabled the child to use tempera, crayon, and chalk on the surface immediately.

For this work William was free to choose any media and materials he could find and use them in any combination and technique he could devise. The objective was to heighten his ability to see the design potentials of a collection of miscellaneous scrap materials as well as the media already in the classroom.

BIRDS WITH NEST
Jennifer Kop, age 10

Tempera and felt-tip ink marker on white drawing paper

The birds were outlined with ink, and the color areas painted with tempera. Surface design and detail were added with marker.

In this version of a subject that appealed to her, Jennifer developed her painting from a beginning sketch of the bird in the center. By the addition of forms and accents that extend the concept and mood, she skillfully used the unpainted surfaces as an integral part of the overall composition.

ENTRANCE TO BISHOP MUSEUM
Noelani Ellis, age 10

Chalk and crayon on white drawing paper

The design of this mixed-media painting was outlined in crayon and colored with chalk.

Working out of doors from an actual scene on the campus, Noelani chose this subject (compare the painting on page 44, left) from a range of scenes that embraced views of Honolulu from sea to mountain, many types of vegetation, and a variety of buildings.

CHRISTMAS TREE
Charlene Kaninau, age 10

Watercolor on white drawing paper

This was painted directly, using a combination of wet color, drybrush, and some dry-on-wet.
   The decorated tree, one of the classic symbols of Christmas, has the same importance to children that pumpkins, turkeys, hearts, and rabbits have in representing other special days. Charlene's painting represents one student's anticipation of the holiday season, its attendant festivities, and vacation.

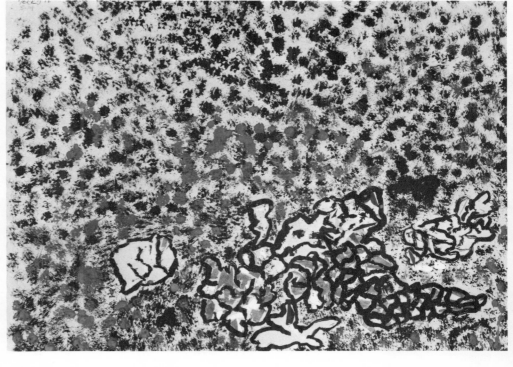

KAMEHAMEHA KARNIVAL
Wynnona Wong, age 10

Opaque watercolor on white drawing paper

The mat effect of this painting was achieved with evenly applied, flat areas, and some dry-on-dry overpainting.

Wynnona made the picture prior to the school carnival that is sponsored yearly by the Parent-Teachers Association. Her images represent the associations provoked by the festival.

DESIGN WITH SMALL SHAPES
Terry Nakamura, age 10

Tempera, india ink, paper, cellophane, and library paste on cream manila paper

The paper areas of this collage were pasted on first, and tempera and india ink were used to enrich the pattern and color.

Terry began by creating a design with several small pieces of paper selected from an assortment of scraps that included many kinds of paper, yarn, and cloth. He worked out from this nucleus to fill most of the picture plane with tempera and ink.

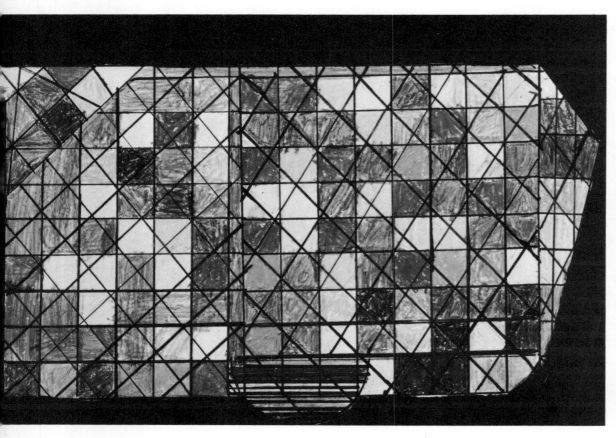

DESIGN OF GEOMETRIC SHAPES
Ronald Perry, age 10

Crayon, india ink, and felt-tip marker on manila tag paper

This composition was planned roughly in pencil on sketch paper. A ruler, triangle, compasses, and ink marker were used to transfer the lines to the lightweight paper, and the resulting pattern was colored with crayon. The surrounding area was done in india ink.

During a study of geometric shapes in mathematics, Ronald noticed the design possibilities of using them in two- and three-dimensional forms. He was delighted to be able to use drawing instruments in creating his design, because the triangle and compasses were new tools for him, and the children seldom use rulers in painting.

When the completed work was pasted on a glass door, Ronald discovered that it was translucent, the color areas seeming to glow in contrast to the almost opaque black.

Paintings by Eleven-year-olds

FIGURES IN MOTION IN SPACE
Kehau Bishaw, age 11

Oil crayon on white drawing paper

To make this painting, varying amounts of crayon were applied to the surface, and some areas were smeared with a finger.

Kehau did this work as part of a limbering-up exercise designed to stimulate free expression and extend her ability to describe figures in motion. By projecting her subject into outer space where there is no gravity and expressing it in an imaginary rather than a realistic manner, the child felt free to "let go," unencumbered by size relationships or preconceived, literal interpretations.

THE BEATLES
Cory Mehau, age 11

Tempera and crayon on white drawing paper

Here, tempera wash was painted over a crayon drawing.

The music created by the group of young men drawn by Cory, their style of dress, and the enormous amount of publicity given them motivated the student to make this statement, which captures the essence of the impression they made on him (compare the painting on page 58, left).

PORTRAIT FROM MODEL
Milton Peter Saffery, age 11

Tempera on glazed paper

This was painted entirely with a small sponge. Milton used a muffin tin as a palette.

Working from a student model in the classroom, the student painted directly on his paper, without preliminary drawing or guidelines. He added the background detail from his own imagination rather than from the actual scene.

BIG EGG
Larry Wong, age 11

Tempera on white drawing paper

The drip effect here was achieved by tilting the
paper while certain colors were still wet. Other
areas were done with rather liquid paint.

The consternation of two very small birds
when confronted by a colossal egg shows the
sense of humor and imagination of the child
who painted this picture during the season
when most of his classmates were painting
traditionally decorated eggs and rabbits.

IMAGERY
Charles Kippen, age 11

Tempera on manila tag paper

This painting was built up of lines and shapes
that were developed with no previous planning
or sketching. The colors used were derived
from the primary colors plus black and white
and were mixed in a plastic egg tray.

An experiment in achieving motion and feeling with line, shape, and color, this picture was
painted as a spontaneous response to an alter-
nation of poetry and music. Short poems and
phrases chosen for their suggestive imagery
were interwoven with brief excerpts of music
selected for mood and tempo.

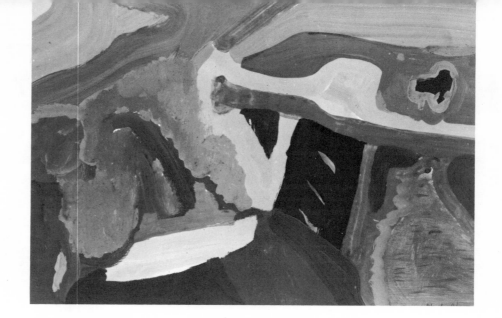

EXPLORER'S SHIP
William Penarosa, age 11

Watercolor and india ink on white manila paper

A preliminary drawing on a small sheet of
sketch paper was transferred freehand to painting paper with ink and a small brush. The design was then painted with moistened watercolor.

The imagination of the child was stirred by
stories of the adventures of explorers of the
New World such as Leif Ericsson, Cartier,
Columbus, and Vespucci, and he expressed
his excitement in this painting.

DESIGN WITH COMPASS
Joseph Chong, age 11

Opaque watercolor on white drawing paper

The cakes of color were moistened with a small amount of water prior to painting. The work combines wet wash and some dry-on-dry.

This design developed from Joseph's discovery that he could insert a short-handled bristle brush in the arm of his compasses and paint circles, which prompted him to create a painting based on circular outlines. He derived great satisfaction from the painting because no one else had thought of the technique.

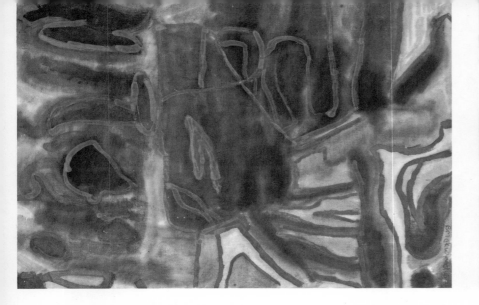

ABSTRACT DESIGN
Brickwood Galuteria, age 11

Cold-water dye and tempera on cloth

Wet-on-wet painting in dye was accented with tempera when partially dry.

In free experimentation with dye effects on cloth, Brickwood added color over color with a manipulative approach until he lost the design he had originally achieved. In order to reestablish his pattern, he tried further application of dye. This was not effective — it served only to compound the lack of shape and color contrast. But by using tempera, which is opaque, he was able to make lines that gave the desired effect.

PORTRAIT
Nani Machida, age 11

Felt-tip ink marker on glass

The outlines of this "stained-glass" painting were planned on sketch paper the same size as the glass. This cartoon was covered with the glass sheet, and the outlines were traced with black marker. The other colors were applied to the reverse side of the glass.

Nani wanted to make this painting as a Christmas present for her parents. The technique was inspired by a display of "stained-glass" paintings done in another class; the idea for the design was selected from a folder of sketches done during the year as voluntary notations and assignments in drawing.

In preparation for this project, Nani became acquainted with some of the traditional and modern uses of stained glass. She did some research in the technical and design problems created when small pieces of glass are set in grooved lead.

Paintings by Twelve-year-olds

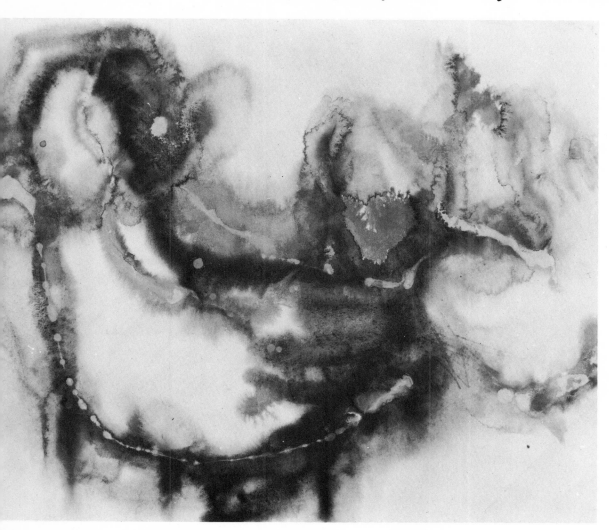

EXPERIMENTAL DESIGN
Lynette Kapahua, age 12

Tempera on white drawing paper

The paper was wet evenly with a saturated sponge, and additional water was dropped on as needed. The paint was applied quickly, with several successive colors overlapping.

Lynette had observed this kind of color effect in the sink during the preparation for painting and in the clean-up period. In her experimental, free painting, she was able to control the color bleeding to some extent, so that she could deliberately achieve a quality she found pleasing.

CORAL IN THE SEA
Stanley Mahoe, age 12

Tempera on white drawing paper

Drybrush painting was used on an unpainted background to produce the texture of the coral. There was some blending of color in the rest of the composition.

Stanley had seen specimens of various kinds of coral in a museum devoted to Hawaiiana. He also had firsthand knowledge of the living growths and skeleton forms of coral that lace the ocean waters along the shore. From this wealth of material, he chose to paint these direct, simple, sculptural forms.

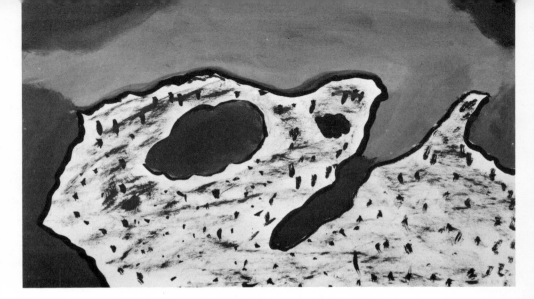

THE EYE
Linda Chang, age 12

Watercolor crayon and india ink on white drawing paper

The initial drawing of this design was done in india ink. Then, one area of the paper at a time was moistened and rubbed with a stick of color. Overpainting was done while the surface was still wet or after adding more water.

After learning facts and seeing illustrative material in a study of the eye, Linda selected the details that seemed essential and translated them into her own graphic conception here.

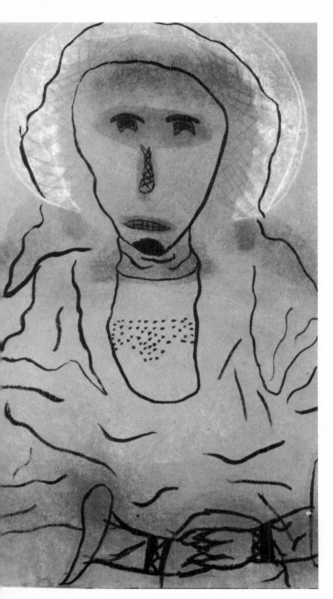

MARY, THE MOTHER OF JESUS
Kimo Warren, age 12

Chalk and india ink on construction paper

Large areas of chalk were applied freely to achieve the general arrangement of shapes that make up the figure. Outlines were drawn over the chalk with india ink and a small brush. Although Kimo made no sketch on the paper prior to painting, he studied the space and knew how he was going to place the figure in it.

Kimo chose to show his interpretation of one of the dominant characters in the story of the life of Christ. He selected Mary as the subject for a sensitive portrait.

GIRL WITH HAT
Healani Mansfield, age 12

Oil paint and turpentine on pebble board

Tube paint was mixed with a small amount of turpentine on a masonite palette for this portrait.

The work was Healani's first essay in oil paint, which was stimulated by the novelty, sophisticated associations, and inviting quality the new medium had for her. She enlarged and adapted part of a drawing from her folder of sketches to fit the dimensions of the available painting surface.

FISHES
Vernon Keawe, age 12

Tempera and felt-tip ink marker on white drawing paper

A thin wash of color was painted over a drawing made with ink markers.

This is one of a profusion of paintings and drawings done by Vernon. It is based on his own experience and his sensitive perception of his surroundings.

Index of Media

COLD-WATER DYE

ABSTRACT DESIGN, 98
IN THE PARK, 72
MARY WITH VEIL, 71
PALM TREE, 73

COLLAGE

COLLAGE WITH CIRCLE, 73
COLLAGE WITH PAINT, 64
DESIGN WITH PAINT AND FINDINGS, 88
DESIGN WITH SMALL SHAPES, 91
SHEPHERD KEEPING WATCH OVER FLOCK, 83
STRING DESIGN WITH TEMPERA, 47

CRAYON

DAY AND NIGHT, 82
FIGURES IN MOTION IN SPACE, 93
WHAT I DID ON THANKSGIVING, 43

FELT-TIP INK MARKER

PORTRAIT, 98

MIXED MEDIA

A CITY WITH BUILDINGS, 49
A DESIGN ABOUT THE CITY, 52
ABORIGINE DESIGN, 61
ABORIGINE WITH BIRDS, 75
BIRDS WITH NEST, 89
BUFFALO ROUND-UP, 66
CLASSMATE, 82
DESIGN, 41
DESIGN OF GEOMETRIC SHAPES, 92
DESIGN ON NEWSPAPER, 45
ENTRANCE TO BISHOP MUSEUM, 89
EXPLORER'S SHIP, 96
FIGURE IN A CIRCLE, 56
FIREWORKS, 76
FISHES, 102
GIANT SQUID, 44
LEAF EATEN BY CATERPILLAR, CLOSE-UP, 57
LINE RHYTHMS DONE TO MUSIC, 68
MARY, THE MOTHER OF JESUS, 101
MEDIEVAL CHURCH, 69
MY SISTER AND I SLEEP IN BUNK BEDS, 85
ONE OF THE THREE KINGS, 63
PAINTING TO MUSIC, HALLOWEEN, 87
SHAKING THE NET, 77
SHIPS AT THE PIER (HONOLULU HARBOR), 73
SPACE MAN, 59
THE BEATLES, 94
THE EYE, 100
THREE CATS, 7 5
TIKI ON KAPA, 84
TURKEY, 50
UNUSUAL ANIMAL, 79
VALENTINE IDEAS, 58

OIL PAINT

GIRL WITH HAT, 101

STRING PAINTING

STRING DESIGN, 66
STRING DESIGN, 64
STRING PAINTING, 63

TEMPERA

A DESIGN, 38
A RAINY DAY, 62
ABORIGINES OF AUSTRALIA, 71
AN OPEN MOUTH, 85
"BEETLE" CLOWN, 58
BIG EGG, 95
BISHOP MUSEUM, 44
BOY WITH GUITAR, 62
CANOE, 65
CORAL IN THE SEA, 100
DESIGN, 39
DESIGN—EXPERIMENTING WITH PAINT, 60
DESIGN—I/T/A SYMBOLS, 47
DESIGN WITH STICK PRINTING, 64
DIAMOND HEAD, 44
EASTER EGG HUNT, 52
EXPERIMENTAL DESIGN, 99
FANTASY, 81
FILLING SPACE, 37
FIRE IN VOLCANO, 70
FOLD-AND-BLOT DESIGN, 46
HAWAIIAN MONARCHS:
    KALAKAUA AND KAMEHAMEHA IV, 78
IMAGERY, 96
JITTERBUGS DANCING, 86
LEI DAY—FLOWERS EVERYWHERE, 53
MOON AND CLOUDS, 70
MOON RISING OVER THE PALI, 69
MUSIC—CITY AND RIVERS, 87
PAINTING TO MUSIC, 81
PAINTING TO MUSIC, 54
POLAR BEAR, 48
PORTRAIT FROM MODEL, 94
SEASHORE, 88
SHIP, 38
SLAVE WORKING ON PLANTATION, 85
SPACE, 81
STATUE OF BUDDHA, 70
THE POLICEMAN, 55
TURKEY, 40
TWO CHIEFS BRING GIFTS TO AN ALII, 88
TWO MEN TALKING, 69
USING BIG BRUSHES, 36
VALENTINE DESIGN WITH LEAVES, 50
WORKING IN RICE PADDY, 80

WATERCOLOR

CHRISTMAS TREE, 90
DESIGN WITH COMPASS, 97
FIRST EXPERIENCE WITH WATERCOLOR, 55
KAMEHAMEHA KARNIVAL, 91

Index of Illustrations

A CITY WITH BUILDINGS, Guy Kaulukukui, 49
A DESIGN, Russell Heirakuji, 38
A DESIGN ABOUT THE CITY, Carla Aiwohi, 52
A RAINY DAY, Kaui Kapele III, 62
ABORIGINE DESIGN, Jeri Baker, 61
ABORIGINE WITH BIRDS, Stephanie Souza, 75
ABORIGINES OF AUSTRALIA, Martha Farrar, 71
ABSTRACT DESIGN, Brickwood Galuteria, 98
AN OPEN MOUTH, Karen Lum, 85
"BEETLE" CLOWN, Mara Gandia, 58
BIG EGG, Larry Wong, 95
BIRDS WITH NEST, Jennifer Kop, 89
BISHOP MUSEUM, Zelda Nishimura, 44
BOY WITH GUITAR, Albert Kam, 62
BUFFALO ROUND-UP, Group work, 66
CANOE, Marcus Rosehill, 65
CHRISTMAS TREE, Charlene Kaninau, 90
CLASSMATE, Edward Kameenui, 82
COLLAGE WITH CIRCLE, Kanani Tirrell, 73
COLLAGE WITH PAINT, Danton Naone, 64
CORAL IN THE SEA, Stanley Mahoe, 100
DAY AND NIGHT, Stephanie Souza, 82
DESIGN, Cindy Caswell, 41
DESIGN, Kolu Kroll, 39
DESIGN—EXPERIMENTING WITH PAINT, Kent Kam, 60
DESIGN—I/T/A SYMBOLS, Stacy Plunkett, 47
DESIGN OF GEOMETRIC SHAPES, Ronald Perry, 92
DESIGN ON NEWSPAPER, Norman Taira, 45
DESIGN WITH COMPASS, Joseph Chong, 97
DESIGN WITH PAINT AND FINDINGS, William Kuhns, 88
DESIGN WITH SMALL SHAPES, Terry Nakamura, 91
DESIGN WITH STICK PRINTING, Colleen Ann Char, 64
DIAMOND HEAD, Lee Ann Toguchi, 44
EASTER EGG HUNT, Michael Soong, 52
ENTRANCE TO BISHOP MUSEUM, Noelani Ellis, 89
EXPERIMENTAL DESIGN, Lynette Kapahua, 99
EXPLORER'S SHIP, William Penarosa, 96
FANTASY, Kim Crowell, 81
FIGURE IN A CIRCLE, James Miura, Jr., 56
FIGURES IN MOTION IN SPACE, Kehau Bishaw, 93
FILLING SPACE, Lehua Novit, 37
FIRE IN VOLCANO, Brant Crabbe, 70
FIREWORKS, Richard Furtado, 76
FIRST EXPERIENCE WITH WATERCOLOR, Herbert Henriques, 55
FISHES, Vernon Keawe, 102
FOLD-AND-BLOT DESIGN, Lilia Carpenter, 46
GIANT SQUID, Hainani Keliikipi, 44
GIRL WITH HAT, Healani Mansfield, 101

HAWAIIAN MONARCHS:
    KALAKAUA AND KAMEHAMEHA IV, Group work, 78
IMAGERY, Charles Kippen, 96
IN THE PARK, Donna Lee Ah Sam, 72
JITTERBUGS DANCING, Noel Smith, 86
KAMEHAMEHA KARNIVAL, Wynnona Wong, 91
LEAF EATEN BY CATERPILLAR, CLOSE-UP, Paul Lucas, 57
LEI DAY—FLOWERS EVERYWHERE, Hainani Keliikipi, 53
LINE RHYTHMS DONE TO MUSIC, Grayling Achiu, 68
MARY, THE MOTHER OF JESUS, Kimo Warren, 101
MARY WITH VEIL, Wesley Kitaoka, 71
MEDIEVAL CHURCH, Mark Duvauchelle, 69
MOON AND CLOUDS, Jo Ann Melemai, 70
MOON RISING OVER THE PALI, George Kahumoku, 69
MUSIC—CITY AND RIVERS, Avis Ing, 87
MY SISTER AND I SLEEP IN BUNK BEDS, Francine Peneku, 85
ONE OF THE THREE KINGS, Mark Furtado, 63
PAINTING TO MUSIC, Karen Chai, 81
PAINTING TO MUSIC, Linda Hutchins, 54
PAINTING TO MUSIC, HALLOWEEN, Kimo Miller, 87
PALM TREE, Nazha Miranda, 73
POLAR BEAR, Keoni Jardine, 48
PORTRAIT, Nani Machida, 98
PORTRAIT FROM MODEL, Milton Peter Saffery, 94
SEASHORE, David Bray, 88
SHAKING THE NET, Bryan Ahue, 77
SHEPHERD KEEPING WATCH OVER FLOCK, Donalei Ho, 83
SHIP, Jon Liu, 38
SHIPS AT THE PIER (HONOLULU HARBOR), Patrick Cullen, 73
SLAVE WORKING ON PLANTATION, Jo-Anne Hugo, 85
SPACE, Faith Kamaka, 81
SPACE MAN, Alvin Baptista, 59
STATUE OF BUDDHA, Barbara Antolin, 70
STRING DESIGN, Group work, 66
STRING DESIGN, Stephen Kauka, 64
STRING DESIGN WITH TEMPERA, Amanda Machado, 47
STRING PAINTING, Paul Lucas, 63
THE BEATLES, Cory Mehau, 94
THE EYE, Linda Chang, 100
THE POLICEMAN, Harding Parilla, Jr., 55
THREE CATS, Elizabeth Bright, 75
TIKI ON KAPA, Gilbert Tam, 84
TURKEY, Douglas Chang, 40
TURKEY, Abraham Klein, 50
TWO CHIEFS BRING GIFTS TO AN ALII, Annette Kama, 88
TWO MEN TALKING, David Yamamoto, 69
UNUSUAL ANIMAL, Hope Ah Loo, 79
USING BIG BRUSHES, Mark Soma, 36
VALENTINE DESIGN WITH LEAVES, Abraham Klein, 50
VALENTINE IDEAS, Wallace Wong, 58
WHAT I DID ON THANKSGIVING, Randall Ishikawa, 43
WORKING IN RICE PADDY, Thyzra Ann Keaweehu, 80